RESEARCH HIGHLIGHTS
IN SOCIAL WORK

Sex, Gender and Care Work

RESEARCH HIGHLIGHTS IN SOCIAL WORK

SEX, GENDER AND CARE WORK

St. Martin's Press

•

Jessica Kingsley *Publishers*

First published in Great Britain in 1987 by Jessica Kingsley Publishers Ltd
21 Aden Grove, London N16 9NP

© 1987 University of Aberdeen, Department of Social Work

British Library Cataloguing in Publication Data
Sex, gender and care work.—(Research
  highlights in social work; 15).
  1. Social service and sex
  I. Horobin, Gordon   II. Series
  361   HV41

  ISBN 1-85302-001-X

First published in the United States of America in 1987 by St. Martin's Press

© 1987 University of Aberdeen, Department of Social Work

All rights reserved. For information, write:
Scholarly & Reference Division,
St. Martin's Press, Inc., 175 Fifth Avenue, New York, NY 10010

Library of Congress Cataloging in Publication Data
Sex, gender, and caring.
  (Research highlights in social work)
  Includes bibliographies and index.
  1. Social service and sex—Great Britain.
2. Sex counseling—Great Britain.   I. Horobin,
Gordon.   II. Series. [DNLM: 1. Counseling.
2. Identification (Psychology)   3. Sex Behavior.
4. Sex Offenses.   BF 692.2   S5183]
HV42.5.S49   1987   306.7   87-9787

  ISBN 0-312-01141-5

Printed and bound in Great Britain by
Biddles Ltd, Guildford and King's Lynn

CONTENTS

Contributors

Gordon Horobin — Taught Sociology at Hull University before joining the MRC Medical Sociology Unit at Aberdeen where he was Assistant Director. He now holds appointments in the Departments of Social Work and of Sociology at Aberdeen and is continuing to carry out research on aspects of General Practice.

Lorraine Gelsthorpe — Currently working in the Institute of Criminology, Cambridge, on an Economic and Social Research Council project on prisons and the prison experiences of staff and prisoners. She has previously worked in psychiatric nursing and residential child care and has also undertaken work on Attendance Centres, inter-agency responses to juvenile crime, alternatives to custody for juveniles, girls' crime and delinquency and the history of prison administration. She has published a number of articles on female crime and justice and on juvenile justice. She edited *Women and Crime* with Allison Morris and has also produced a training tape and material for practitioners in this area. She is currently preparing a book on sexism, crime and justice.

Elizabeth Hall — Elizabeth Hall studied Psychology at Newcastle University, and completed research into the intellectual functioning of the elderly for a doctorate before training to be a clinical psychologist at Newcastle and Aberdeen. She is now Senior Clinical Psychologist with Grampian Health Board and obtained the Diploma in Psychotherapy at Aberdeen University in 1985. She has particular interests in gender-related effects on psychotherapy, sexual abuse and bereavement. She is co-author of a book, *Intellectual Functioning of the Aged*, published in 1973.

Keith White — Keith White is a practising residential care worker at Mill Grove, an extended foster family with a history spanning three generations. He is also a part-time lecturer in sociology at Spurgeons College, London. He is a past president of the Social Care Association and vice-chairman of the National Council of Voluntary Child Care Organisations. He has contributed regularly to both *Social Work Today* and *Community*

Care and his publications include *A Place for Us* (1976), *Caring for Deprived Children* (1979), *Why Care?* (1980), *The Best of In Residence*, Vols I and II. He was residential child care representative on the Barclay Committee.

Linda Coley

Linda Coley has worked in a variety of day and residential settings for people with mental handicaps. She is now Head of Home for a residential unit in the London Borough of Camden offering accommodation for people with a mild handicap and 'outreach' work to others living in their own accommodation. She has worked with many individuals on packages of information and counselling on sexuality and is currently Co-ordinator of the Camden Group in Sexuality which has produced comprehensive guidelines to staff on how to respond to the sexuality of people with mental handicaps.

Richard Marler

Richard Marler has worked in day, residential and field work settings with people with varying degrees of handicap. He was co-ordinator of social work with residential units for the Spastics Society before moving to Camden, initially as Development Officer and then as organiser of the Special Needs Unit for adults with multiple handicaps. He was co-leader of 'self-awareness' groups and worked closely with Linda Coley in the co-ordinating group on the production of staff guidelines. He is now senior social worker on a community mental handicap team in West Sussex.

Bobbie Fraser

Bobbie Fraser trained in social work. Her early practical experience was with children and families in a range of settings and later with adults in the Department of Psychiatry, Western General Hospital, Edinburgh. She undertook additional training in marital and sexual counselling and is currently part-time teacher in the Department of Social Policy and Social Work at Edinburgh University. She also does sexual and marital counselling, on a sessional basis, with Lothian Family Conciliation Service.

Siobhan Lloyd

Siobhan Lloyd is lecturer in Social Work (social policy and community work) at Aberdeen University.

She was previously a community worker in Liverpool. She has recently completed a research project funded by Social Services Group on alternatives to custody for drunkenness offenders and is currently undertaking research jointly with Liz Hall into professional responses to, and training for, work with adults who have experienced sexual abuse as children.

Derek Perkins

Derek Perkins is Chief Psychologist at Broadmoor Hospital. After graduating from University College, London, in 1969 he joined the Prison Department as psychologist at Birmingham Prison. He then qualified in clinical psychology and went on to work as Senior, and then Principal, Clinical Psychologist at Swinfen Hall Youth Custody Centre, Birmingham Prison and the Midland Centre for Forensic Psychiatry. He has worked for over 15 years on the institutional and community treatment of sex offenders, and has published a number of articles and book chapters on this subject and was a member of the Howard League Working Party on sex offenders, which published its findings in the book *Unlawful Sex* in 1983.

Ann Fillmore

Ann Fillmore is a behavioural scientist and has worked for over ten years with victims of violence. In 1976 she helped establish the first crisis phone line for battered women in Los Angeles, along with one of the first battered women's shelters. In London she worked as a child abuse investigator and later, in Sweden, became a private consultant on the problems of victims. Her research into the phenomenon of the Stockholm Syndrome and traumatic bonding is known internationally and she is presently finishing her PhD in international relations with the University of Aberdeen, studying the personality of the terrorist. Her present work in Oregon involves the treatment of dual status youth, especially sex offenders, as well as other victims of violence.

Coralie Jewell

Coralie Jewell is therapist and assistant director at the Center for Behavioural Intervention, coordinating and facilitating conjoint couples therapy with adult sex offenders and their spouses. She runs support groups for spouses of sexual offenders and treatment groups for female victims of sexual assault. Previously she was the education/media coordinator for Alternatives to Sexual Abuse, which is a foundation providing training for professionals in the field. As an adolescent and family therapist in one of Oregon's residential treatment centers for delinquent youth, she dealt with male victims of sexual abuse and their families.

Reg Vernon

Reg Vernon is a member of the Intake Team of Colchester Social Services. Previously he followed a career in the printing industry but changed course to study at Plater College, Oxford. He then read for an MA (Hons) degree at Dundee University followed by his CQSW training at Aberdeen University, whence he went to Colchester.

Editorial

Gordon Horobin

'Sex' is an awkward word, with too many meanings and connotations for easy precision. This is not simply a matter of looseness in usage, for the ambiguities reflect a real interrelatedness in ways of thinking, speaking and acting. Conventionally, 'sex' has to do with the distinction between male and female, with 'gender' referring to masculine and feminine, but, however careful we may try to be in separating the biological from the social, we frequently fail. This is not, of course, to deny the fundamental importance of the distinction: gender, the social characteristics and expectations of male and female, is very variable across time and place, having little to do with biological differences but much to do with structures of power within societies.

But 'sex' is also used as a shorthand term for all the complex associations of both sex and gender, including sexual behaviour, sexual relationships, sexual mores and sexuality itself. All of these themes are discussed in this book but, equally, there are many more issues of gender, sex and sexuality which have been omitted. The choice of subjects and their ordering within the book may well appear arbitrary and idiosyncratic. I make no apology for this: the finished product reflects the interests of authors, editorial advisers and the editor, as well as a sizeable element of opportunism! It could hardly be otherwise.

In the first chapter, Gelsthorpe shows how laws which are sex-neutral in form are often discriminatory in enforcement, interpretation, and application. This is perhaps inevitable in a sphere of social life where imputations of motive and character abound. Whereas the delinquent behaviour of boys is often seen as symptomatic of 'a phase' of life, an exaggerated form of rehearsing masculine roles, similarly unlawful acts committed by girls are more often interpreted as evidence of emotional disturbance. In consequence, female offenders may be treated more leniently, so long as they exhibit socially approved remorse and non-aggressive responses. If sex-role expectations are breached, however, such paternalistic tolerance is withdrawn. The differential emphasis on boys' deeds and girls' needs raises the question of whether justice requires equal treatment or equal provision.

Differential expectations of and responses to the behaviour of men and women are also discussed in Hall's paper on psychotherapy. Here the models or theories may be implicit rather than explicit and are consequently more resistant to examination. Nevertheless, Hall provides ample evidence of the impact of gender on therapeutic relationships. The research literature shows that male therapists are judged incapable of empathising fully with female clients, while male clients have difficulty in admitting to or demonstrating those emotional responses adjudged to be 'female'. The sexuality of female clients may be feared by some male therapists, while others may encourage or give undue attention to sexual talk by clients. Hall discusses recent trends in the acknowledgement and uses of transference and countertransference in therapy and concludes that issues of gender and sexual identity can never be ignored in therapeutic relationships. She also warns us to beware of making adjustment to stereotypical sex roles the goal of therapy.

In the next three chapters, the focus is on sexual relationships. Such relationships in residential settings have become an emotionally loaded subject in recent times, although the ethics of encouraging or discouraging, permitting or punishing sexual behaviour in these institutional settings have always been contentious. White notes that the trend towards making residential 'homes' more 'family-like' ought to lead to a dispassionate, or even better, a compassionate, discussion of appropriate taboos on 'incest' in such quasi-families. In the aftermath of the Kincora investigations, even acknowledgement of the possibility of sexual attachments between residents and staff seems to have disappeared. While this may protect residents from unwelcome sexual advances at least in the short term, fear of the consequences may now inhibit even the most innocent, and potentially therapeutic, display of affection between staff and resident.

Coley and Marler, as co-authors of a thoughtful and humane set of guidelines on sexual relationships in settings for people with mental handicaps, have continued their discussion here. The declaration of the handicapped person's right to sexual fulfilment, which we would surely all endorse, carries with it a need to face issues of great sensitivity and poignancy. On the one hand is the desire to 'normalise' the social life and interactions of those with handicaps. Yet the settings in which they live, whether residential or 'in the community', are not conducive to 'normal' privacy. Unfortunately, sheltering normally implies a degree of communal living and surveillance. Where, then, and in what circumstances, can normal sexual relationships develop? And there is still, of course, the enormously difficult question of informed consent: the temptation is strong for staff to play safe and, by acting *in loco parentis*, prevent sexual relationships from developing. The involvement of the staff, themselves, in sexual encounters with residents is an even more difficult issue, but one which receives little discussion.

Sexual relationships in other residential homes, especially those for the elderly, have not been subjected to the same sorts of investigation, and subsequent publicity, as establishments for young people or people with handicaps. Yet the elderly, too, have sexual needs, and staff as well as the governing bodies may seek to encourage, facilitate, discourage or prevent expression of those needs. It had been intended to include, in this volume, a chapter on this theme but it proved impossible to commission one within the time available. Pauline Woodard, officer in charge of an elderly persons' Residential Home in the West Country, has given me permission to quote from her letter to me on this topic.

'I feel that residential care is to some extent institutionalised, and this cannot be helped, even though we may try to make [the home] as "home-like" as possible. But there do have to be some rules. Sex, in residential care, should be catered for, and privacy to enjoy each other's company is essential. Inside that elderly man or woman is a young person, with the same feelings about falling in love and making relationships. This is so often ignored or looked on, by some, as wrong, inappropriate or even dirty. It is an area which I try to bring to the attention of staff and to allow for. Last week, a very lively lady resident was seen "frolicking" with a gentleman resident in the hallway of the Home. It was suggested that more privacy would be found in her bedroom, whereupon they took up the suggestion. That night the lady had a stroke and a heart-attack, and died next day. I have since pondered upon the "risk-taking" that I had encouraged, but have now come to terms with it, having remembered the smile on her face when she died. What a way to go!'

Further editorial comment upon this anecdote, other than to thank Pauline Woodard for allowing me to use it, would be superfluous!

Fraser's chapter deals with a rather different topic, that of sexual counselling. Sexual difficulties are widespread in Western societies and certainly figure prominently in marital discord and breakdown. Despite this, development of specialised counselling has been slow and haphazard in Britain, with most problems being ignored or, at best, ventilated in medical consultations or in marriage guidance. Inadequate sex education is one factor in the prevalence of problems and it is inevitable that most parental opposition to improved education comes from those parents who are inhibited by their own unacknowledged difficulties. Fraser shows, in her discussion of the research literature, that specialised counselling is effective in a high proportion of cases, but is dependent both on the nature of the problem and the quality of the relationship between the couple. It is, perhaps, somewhat surprising that the use of surrogate partners in therapy seems to be limited to one centre in Britain, given the sizeable proportion of individuals, as distinct from couples, seeking help. There are complicated ethical and legal issues involved, however. Fraser concludes with an important warning to helpers not to impose their own, probably egalitarian, model of 'ideal' sexual relationships on clients. To do so may well demonstrate a desire to help and improve the client's relationship but it may equally be inappropriate to the client's situation.

The final section of the book is devoted to overt problems that have a sexual component, even if they are not, of themselves, sexual problems. Rape, for example, as Lloyd points out, is a crime of violence, with sex as the mode or weapon. Nevertheless the sexual nature of the crime, and its basis in gender relations, serve to demarcate it from other violent acts. Feminist reactions to the haphazard, ineffectual and often damaging ways in which rape has been dealt with by conventional police and court procedures, have led to the institution of rape crisis centres. In some instances, relationships between such groups or agencies and the police are poor or hostile, while in others they are mutually supportive. There is a manifest need for specialist teams within police departments, a trend much more evident in the USA than in Britain, and it is unfortunate that such specialisation is only possible in large, urban centres. The needs of incest survivors are, perhaps, even more special and the caring response demands careful examination of the participants' own attitudes towards sex, sex roles and sexuality. And rape also demands that attention be paid to the wider institutional and societal context in which it is embedded.

The two papers by Perkins and Fillmore and Jewell are concerned with treatment programmes for sex offenders in Britain and in the USA. Perkins notes that a variety of offences and of offenders demands a variety of models of practice. Intervention may be aimed at one or more of:– the motivations of the offender, the offender's internal inhibitors, the external inhibitors or at enhancing the victims' resistance. The latter is a contentious issue, of course, especially if attention is focused there by strictures from police or judges on the need for women to avoid 'provocative' dress or demeanour! It is important to reaffirm the responsibility of the offender for his acts, and to treat with suspicion such rationalisations or accounts as 'I have a greater need for sex than other men', or 'I thought it [incest] was better than going with another woman'. Such accounts, however, insofar as they may be 'real' to the offender, can have causal significance and must be addressed in treatment.

Fillmore and Jewell report on a specialised treatment programme for offenders and attempt to evaluate it. The programme is described in detail as are the measurements used during treatment. Important elements here are the combination of physical measurements and psychological assessments, and the necessity of building into treatment more general social skills.

The final chapter deals with some aspects of what has become the 'moral panic' of the late '80s, AIDS. The question is raised of how can social workers, without specialised knowledge, work with AIDS victims and, just as importantly, their partners and other 'kin'. That AIDS is, so far, primarily associated, in the West, with homosexuality and/or with intravenous drug usage, gives it a deeply stigmatised image which may well get in the way of effective, non-judgmental counselling. It is, of course, the combination of the stigma and the incurability of the condition that is likely to create problems for the helper. Nevertheless, it is the ordinary – if indeed they are ordinary – skills of bereavement counselling for partners and support for the dying client, that are needed here. As with programmes for sex offenders, discussed in earlier papers, so with AIDS victims, acknowledgement of responsibility is quite compatible with sympathetic helping.

Overall, the reader may well find this a mixed bag of offerings. However, to return to the theme raised at the outset, all the papers demonstrate the inter-relatedness of sex, gender and sexuality. Relationships between the sexes (or, indeed, within one sex) always involve notions of gender and sex roles, and problems are most likely to occur if these notions are not shared between the partners. Similarly, the ways in which we conceptualise gender and sex roles always involve, implicitly or explicitly, notions of and feelings about our sexuality.

The Differential Treatment of Males and Females in the Criminal Justice System

Loraine Gelsthorpe

The subject of discrimination in law and practice has long been recognised as a legitimate focus of study. Initial interest in this area was prompted by a concern over whether women were being treated equally or fairly in both private domestic spheres and the public domain of education, employment, industry and the state. There are numerous texts which exemplify this interest and arguments have been well documented by Atkins and Hoggett [1] for instance, and by Reid and Wormald [2].

Although discrimination remains a concern, more recent analyses have adopted a different approach, becoming less preoccupied with instances of discrimination and an insistence on 'equal' treatment, and more interested in the way in which the law may operate to reproduce a social order which is based upon a system of inequality or oppression. The work of Mary Evans and Clare Ungerson [3], Eva Gamarnikow et al. [4], Carol Smart [5] and Critical Social Policy writers [6] is all important here in describing how discrimination is not simply conducted through the law mechanically, but is expressed in everyday activities which are shaped by the law. This leads to studies of socialisation processes and to studies of the family as being derived from a patriarchal view of the world, for instance. The aim of this chapter, however, is to introduce the reader to research findings from studies of discrimination, to summarise some of the key issues and, where appropriate, to draw implications for policy and practice.

I have chosen two main areas upon which to concentrate within the broad context of sex, gender and caring: gender issues in criminal justice and gender issues in juvenile justice. As a preliminary, however, I wish to make three general points. The first concerns the fact that consideration of discrimination in the criminal and juvenile justice systems cannot be divorced from discrimination in other spheres of life; the spheres are interrelated [7].

My second point also concerns the issue of discrimination. Focus on discrimination has more often than not been prompted by a concern for women and girls and whether they are being treated equally or fairly, but discrimination does not always work one way, nor does it apply to *all* females. This chapter is primarily based on research which focuses on the treatment of women and girls in these systems, but enough is known about practices to suggest that not all females are equally subject to scrutiny; race [8], home circumstances [9], and perhaps even characteristics of appearance and demeanour [10] are all mediating factors. Gender issues cannot be considered in isolation.

My third point is essentially that it is not always appropriate to draw distinctions between images and understandings of adult female offenders and juvenile female offenders. This follows the arguments of Hudson [11] that theories about female offenders generally lack an age perspective. What this means is that commentators have rarely conceived of female delinquency as a distinctive phase in females' lives, unlike male delinquency which is often viewed as part of adolescence [12,13,14]. Commentators on women and girls more typically describe delinquency in terms of a gender perspective. There is then a rather false distinction drawn between the criminal justice and juvenile justice sections in this chapter. However, in the first section I make reference to general concepts, models and research findings as well as the specific treatment of adults, and some of these general models have relevance for the consideration of juveniles. In the second section I concentrate on the actual treatment of boys and girls in the juvenile justice system.

Most of the research material and practice evidence used in this chapter relates to England and Wales and the USA though the general ideas and principles are relevant in Scotland.

GENDER ISSUES IN CRIMINAL JUSTICE

One of the first issues to address here is of course that the law does not affect males and females in the same way. Indeed it may seem that the behaviour of males is more readily criminalised than that of females. Only men may be charged with an offence relating to indecent exposure, for example. But equivalent behaviour by females would be *covered* by the law even if not *framed* in law (causing a breach of the peace, for instance). Similarly, whereas only males can be charged with the offence of rape, females could be charged with the offence of indecent assault.

Most laws are sex neutral in their language, but their enforcement may be discriminatory. Criminal statistics, for instance, suggest that prostitution is predominantly a crime committed by women; male prostitutes and male clients were, until recently, rarely criminalised [15].

The literature on discrimination in the Criminal Justice System itself is diverse, but four main models can be identified.

(a) *Preferential Treatment*: the assumption here is that a woman is dealt with more leniently than a man. She is thought to be less likely to be arrested or convicted. The underlying rationale is male chivalry or simply practicality due to woman's child-care responsibilities.

It has long been supposed that female offenders meet with more favourable treatment at the hands of the law enforcement agencies than males, and the leniency factor has been particularly emphasised in attempts to explain the relatively low recorded incidence of female crime. Some research has addressed the nature of victims' responses to female offenders. Hindelang [16] examined American victimisation data between 1972-1976. He found that the victims of female offenders did report them less often to the police than was true for the victims of male offenders. But this difference in victims' referral rates could well be explained by differences in the nature of the offences committed by men and women. Further, when the sex of the victim was controlled for, there was no support for the idea that male victims did not report female offenders. Indeed, if there was any preferential treatment, it was shown by female and not male victims.

The nature of the offence is clearly a determining factor in decisions whether or not to report offenders. Previously Cameron [17], in her shoplifting research, had demonstrated that fewer women were referred to the police by department stores than men (though the disparity was not as marked for black women). Hindelang [18] however, found that although there was some bias in favour of women in the early 1960s, this had disappeared by 1968. The decision to report was then related to the value of the object stolen, what was stolen and the method of theft.

The police, too, have wide discretion in both the interpretation of the law and in responses to suspects or offenders. At face value, the Criminal Statistics suggest that the police are lenient towards women since relatively few of them appear as known offenders. Indeed, the ratio of males to females found guilty of indictable offences (all courts) in 1984 was 6:1, and cautioning statistics suggest further leniency.

TABLE 1

Offenders cautioned for indictable offences as a percentage of persons found guilty or cautioned, by sex and age, 1984

	Males %	Females %
10<14	75	91
14<17	45	71
17 and over	5	14
All ages	20	35

(Home Office, Criminal Statistics, England & Wales)

Not only do we not know the real extent of crime committed by women [19] but statistics can be explained in other ways. Studies of police discretion [20,21] stress the importance of demeanour and attitude in interactions with the police. Clearly this is relevant for both sexes, but it is plausible that because of differential socialisation processes, females are more likely to demonstrate the behaviour expected by the police than males. De Fleur, for instance, suggests that stereotypical feminine behaviour is likely to provoke a sympathetic response in male officers [10]. There is also some evidence [22] to suggest that girls are more favourably disposed to the police than boys. The police are also less likely to arrest non-serious, non-persistent offenders [23] and women are more likely than men to fall into this category.

Interestingly, the number of women in the police force has increased since the 1950s and this itself could have affected the processing of female suspects. One can only speculate about the effect of this but since women are inclined to be more censorious of each other [24] it is possible that this may have led to changes in the processing of female offenders. There is also evidence which indicates that girls who commit what are known in the USA as 'status offences' (promiscuity, truancy, running away and so on) are dealt with more harshly by the police [25,26]. Race and class are likely to influence police decisions too. Visher [27] has suggested that black and working class women are less likely to be dealt with preferentially than white and middle class women. Nagel [28] believes the issue to be complex too and she refers to the effect of marital status in her analysis of 'preferential treatment' with married women (who conform to the sex role stereotype) faring better than single women. Farrington and Morris [29], in one of the most methodologically sound studies yet, carried out a survey of the sentencing of offenders convicted of theft in Cambridge and found that women did appear to be more leniently dealt with than men. Again, sex was not related to sentencing severity independently of other factors but they found that certain factors were influencing sentences for women which did not influence the sentences given to men, namely marital status, having children and expressions of remorse. Thomas [30] cites many cases to support the influence of having children upon sentencing, and similarly Mary Eaton [31] describes in some detail how the family is central to pleas of mitigation offered on behalf of men and women – though because of prevailing ideology relating to 'appropriate cases' courtroom practice generally works to the advantage of women and disadvantage of men.

Carlen [32] who interviewed sheriffs (judges) in Scotland, takes this argument further since she reveals that decisions over whether or not to imprison depends upon whether women might be classed as 'good mothers' or 'failed mothers'.

It is still unclear as to whether or not there is preferential treatment for females, decision-making depends on conformity to traditional role stereotypes. It may be that preferential treatment is reserved for passive, remorseful, unaggressive females. Indeed, it would be interesting to monitor the effect on victims and the police of increasing assertiveness amongst women.

(b) *Paternalistic Treatment*: this implies a need to protect women from their environment and from themselves. Paradoxically, this can result in increased intervention in the lives of women and girls and in the incarceration of them.

The argument is essentially that, as children are treated by parents, so women are seen as needing support on the basis that they are powerless and propertyless. They are also seen as needing guidance and control since they are not fully responsible and not able to judge their own 'best interests'. The suggestion here is that the criminal law and its enforcement both reflect and ensure the continuance of women's position as a powerless and propertyless social group. The point can be illustrated by Pearson's account of the treatment of women defendants in three British magistrates' courts [33]. Claiming that women are treated as 'quasi juveniles', she reflects that two models are employed to deal with them, a 'mental illness' model and a 'social casualty' model. This response, whilst seemingly humane and sensitive to the problems of the women concerned (for example, those on low incomes, often on social security, often heads of one parent families with dependent children, commonly charged with a form of theft such as shoplifting, meter breaking, false social security claims) is seen by Pearson as reflecting and reinforcing their difficult position. Yet 'soft' treatment and a reluctance to imprison such women, leaves the roots of their problems untouched. Clearly, although individual women may benefit, the general effect is oppressive. Susan Edwards, in her 1984 study of Women on Trial [34] offers further illustration of paternalistic treatment of women in her findings that women are more likely to be remanded for medical or psychiatric reports – as if women cannot possibly have committed offences in a rational way (though it is not always magistrates who decide to order reports, it is often solicitors who are instrumental in this). Evidence offered as illustration of the differential response to boys and girls in the juvenile court is also relevant to discussion here. As I shall explain later in the chapter, perceptions of behaviour often lead practitioners and decision-makers to concern themselves with girls' social and sexual behaviour as well as (in some cases instead of) their offending behaviour. This paternalistic response to girls often results in them being incarcerated even if it is done in their own 'best interests' [35,36,37,38]. DHSS figures reveal that a disproportionate number of girls are received into care on the grounds that they are in moral danger and figures supplied by the Scottish Office on the Children's Hearing System also reflect a prevailing paternalistic attitude towards girls. Though fewer girls than boys are referred into the system a much higher proportion of them will proceed to hearings. Once in the system girls have a higher chance of being placed under compulsory measures of care, particularly residential care in cases of non-offence grounds concerning their general social conduct. Warren [39] has calculated that boys entering the CHS in Scotland have a one in 12 chance of having a residential supervision order imposed. For girls it is one in nine.

(c) *Harsh Treatment*: in this model certain women (for example, aggressive women) are given harsher treatment than other women and possibly men). Indeed what becomes clear here is that some women may not only be punished for their offending behaviour but also for their breach of sex-role expectations [40]. The thesis is reminiscent of the 'evil woman' idea given forceful expression in the Italian proverb that 'rarely is a woman wicked, but when she is she surpasses the man.'

Cockburn and Maclay [41], May [42] and Wadsworth [43] all suggest that girls brought to court have committed fewer offences than their male counterparts and indeed are more likely to be placed in some kind of institutional care for these offences. However May [42] makes an important clarification of this 'evil woman' thesis. He notes that girls who do end up in the courts are likely to be perceived as constituting a more serious problem than the average male delinquent simply because female offenders may be subject to much finer filtering procedures, by the police, for instance. Simon's [40] thesis has to be viewed in the light of this.

Nevertheless, Worrall [44] advances the idea that females are not necessarily leniently treated and in some circumstances harsh treatment may ensue; she uses the notion of 'incongruity' to explain this. A woman who enters the criminal justice system is incongruous – she is out of place, a man is not. Thus it may be argued that this serves to define acceptable behaviour for women in a restrictive way and breaches are severely penalised. Providing that women act their part within the limits imposed by the traditional image of women they are not seen as 'criminal'.

Research on the composition of magistrates' benches is also of interest here. Farrington and Morris [29] and Dominelli [45] suggest that female magistrates are harsher on female offenders than male magistrates though differences were not quite statistically significant.

Again, it would be interesting to monitor effects upon courtroom responses and sentencing of women's increasing assertiveness and perhaps changing image. Indeed, it is possible though not yet demonstrable through hard data, that as women have struggled to free themselves from 'traditional' classifications and images, there has been an anti-feminist backlash within the courtroom resulting in harsher treatment for women. (Some of the women from Greenham Common and other female peace protestors would certainly want to claim this). As women's roles change they are perhaps seen to contribute to a general lessening and removal of 'civilised standards' and thus to merit harsh rather than lenient treatment [46].

(d) *Equal Treatment*: In this model it is assumed that sex is irrelevant in decision-making within the criminal justice system and that for similar offences males and females have an equal probability of arrest, conviction and incarceration. Research is scant here, though Thomas [30] concludes from his study of sentencing patterns and the principles of sentencing that in the main males and females are subject to equal treatment.

Some early work in the USA suggested, in the wake of notions about chivalry towards females, that girls were equally liable to arrest if they resisted police approaches or ran away. But there has been little research on this issue.

There is a common thread which runs through research in this field. Preferential, paternalistic and harsh treatment of females are all linked to the promotion and perpetuation of the status quo – and traditional sex role stereotypes. The actual treatment of men and women within the penal system confirms the idea that there are distinctive images of men and women. Women in prison, for instance, are allowed their own clothes and the regime is more relaxed than in the men's prisons [47]. Indeed plans were introduced for a new 'psychiatric prison' in the 1960s since it was assumed that women's psychological needs were paramount and that women offenders must be 'disturbed' in some way. But these plans were overtaken by rising numbers and a tougher, political approach. Nevertheless, there is some evidence to support claims that even in this sphere women are treated as 'quasi-juveniles' [32].

The issues which are apparent here recur throughout the chapter. Females are clearly different from males. The crucial question is how much this matters for participation in the law, the criminal justice and penal systems. Biological differences cannot be denied but the issue is the social use made of these and whether this use is unjust or invidious. Is paternalism based on real differences so that it amounts to 'justice as fairness', or merely on perceived differences? Where perceived differences are spurious or invidious, differential responses to males and females are unfair and unjust. Like penalties to women and men for like offences provide what might be termed 'paper justice.' But in terms of 'real justice' or 'justice as fairness' one would have to consider the effects of particular penalties upon men and women. The impact of imprisonment may be greater on women than on men, for instance, because of their domestic responsibilities; to take heed of this is to perpetuate the status quo and inequality; to ignore the fact is to subject the woman's family to suffering and hardship. In other words, does equal treatment necessarily mean 'just' or 'fair' treatment? Moreover, in what circumstances is it permissible or acceptable for those who work within the criminal justice system to promote differential responses to offenders when differential responses to date have been based on images of males and females which are necessary to perpetuate the status quo?

GENDER ISSUES IN JUVENILE JUSTICE

The treatment of 'difficult' or 'delinquent' boys and girls has not always been differentiated, but from the 18th century onwards there is considerable evidence of increasing demands for both separate and different responses to them. Such demands were frequently accompanied by comments and claims that girls were more difficult to 'rescue' than boys, and special missions and societies were set up, not to punish the girls per se, but to instil good virtues in them, to 'raise a consciousness in them' [48]. Mary Carpenter, inveterate critic of the penal system adopted for juvenile delinquents argued all the more strongly that the existing system (whereby many juveniles were imprisoned) was iniquitous when it was used for girls [49]. The system which was needed to reclaim them was a 'wise and kind system.' Indeed, in so far as the Reformatory and Industrial Schools offered 'care' for those admitted to them, it is clear that one of the prime objects of such care was to teach boys and girls their respective duties [50]. Girls were to become home-makers and mothers and boys home providers, and steps towards these roles were perceived to be steps towards redemption.

Perceptions of the differential needs of boys and girls were also reflected in the setting up of Borstal Institutions and Approved Schools. In a report of the Association of Headmasters, Headmistresses and Matrons of Approved Schools, for instance, it is made clear that girls' admission to such schools was primarily due to prostitution and sex offences [51]. Their 'needs' were, as a consequence, for medical treatment (in many cases) and for an emotional security which would divert their attention from sexual activities. Moreover, in designing schools and school policy it was seen as desirable to take note of the fact that 'girls appreciate the value of a homely atmosphere' [51], girls were viewed as 'less gregarious than boys' and the report continues, 'delinquent girls are particularly individualistic' and 'sex problems cause a great deal of worry and the hysterical, truculent or destructive girl tends to behave in a dramatic manner' [51,52].

Continuing these themes Annelise Walker [53], for instance, clearly saw girls as 'vulnerable'. She viewed girls' behaviour as 'wayward' more than 'observably delinquent' as in the case of boys and went on to argue that it was predominantly inter-personal conflicts which characterised and precipitated girls' entrance to the criminal justice system and thus that 'relationship building' ought to feature in the response to girls.

Interestingly, the Advisory Council on the Penal System stressed the psychological problems of girls in their 1968 recommendation to the government that the only existing detention centre for girls should be closed without replacement. They concluded:

'We are sure that the detention centre concept is not appropriate for girls' [54]

and argued that

'the needs of delinquent boys and girls are so dissimilar that there is no reason why disposals open to the courts should be the same for both sexes' [54].

Girls in trouble, it was said, are

'usually unhappy and disturbed, often sexually promiscuous and often rejected by their families. They are usually in great need of help and understanding however reluctant to accept sympathy and affection they may appear to be' [54].

It is indeed significant that the Criminal Justice Act (1982) and the rearrangement and renaming of resources which it has entailed has not changed the disparities in custodial provisions for males and females. The Act has not re-introduced detention centres for girls and this is somewhat surprising given the apparent increases in girls' crime. Presumably the detention centre concept with its primary emphasis on control and on providing a 'short, sharp shock' for miscreants is still thought to be inappropriate for girls.

Information about 'perceived needs' of girls and views about their 'just deserts' can also be usefully gleaned from statistical analyses of sentencing patterns. Not only are females more likely than males to be cautioned by the police rather than proceeded against, but figures reveal a greater tendency to deal with girls by way of conditional discharges, fines and supervision.

TABLE 2

Percentage of persons aged 10 and under 14 sentenced for indictable offences who received various sentences by sex and type of sentence or order in England and Wales

Percentage of total persons sentenced

Sex and year	Abs. or cond. disch.	Super-vision Order	Fine	Att. Centre Order	Care Order	O/wise dealt with	Total
1984							
MALES	39	18	17	20	5	1	100
FEMALES	46	24	21	4	4	1	100

(Drawn from Home Office Criminal Statistics, England and Wales).

TABLE 3

Percentage of persons aged 14 and under 17 sentenced for indictable offences who received various sentences by sex and type of sentence or order in England and Wales

Percentage of total persons sentenced

Sex and year	Abs.or cond. disch.	Super-vision Order	Fine	Comm. Serv. Order	Att. Cent. Order	Det. Cent. Order	Care Ord.	Bor. tr./ Y.Cus.	O/wise dealt with	Total
1984										
MALES	22	17	27	3	16	8	2	4	1	100
FEMALES	37	21	28	1	7	*	3	2	1	100

(Drawn from Home Office Statistics, England and Wales, 1984) (* not applicable)

The Scottish system too reflects a differential perception of needs (Scottish Office statistics on Children's Hearing Disposals).

Of course, offence patterns are important here in accounting for sentencing, but the general 'casework' approach to female offenders suggests that consideration of their supposed psychological needs and motivations tends to be uppermost in the minds of sentencers and practitioners.

Contemporary literature reveals four main themes which guide responses to boys and girls in the juvenile criminal justice system and allied agencies. Firstly, that most boys offend at some point during their adolescence; it is viewed as a part of their growing up and most (though clearly not all) grow out of it [55]. In contrast, in view of the fact that relatively few girls commit crimes (or so it seems) it is assumed that those who do must be abnormal in some way. Cowie, Cowie and Slater, for instance, although not assuming the causes of crime to be solely within the realm of physiology, see physical characteristics as predisposing factors towards crime. They report

> 'delinquent girls more often than boys have other forms of impaired physical health; they are noticed to be oversized, lumpish, uncouth and graceless, with a varied incidence of minor physical defects' [56].

Secondly, whereas most boys' delinquency is property-related (theft, burglary, taking and driving away), it is assumed that girls' delinquency is very often sexual delinquency. Frequently we hear the cries that girls are 'at risk' and in 'moral danger'. Casburn [37], Shacklady-Smith [57] and Campbell [58], for example, all provide evidence for this and, as stated,

DHSS Local Authority Statistics reflect that a disproportionate number of girls are in care on these grounds.

TABLE 4

Children who came into care under 1969 CYP Act Sections 1(2); 1(2)d; 1(2)f or 7(7) during the 12 months ended March 31 expressed as a percentage (all ages)

	Boys %	Girls %	Total (=100%)
1(2)c Moral Danger	27	73	146 cases
1(2)d Beyond Control	53	47	623
1(2)f or 7(7) Offence	85	15	2,113

DHSS Local Authority Statistics, England, 1983.

Linked to this theme is a third common observation that delinquent girls come from broken homes more often than delinquent boys. Thus their delinquency (sexual or otherwise) is largely attributable to deficient family relationships. Much of the research here suggests that it is girls' need to seek compensatory affectional responses outside the home which leads to their delinquent or difficult behaviour. Morris [59], for instance, argues that since the focal concerns of females are more intimately linked to the family situation in contrast to the concerns of boys which lie outside of the home, frustrations and disappointments in this sphere are likely to encourage a reaction which may be manifested in delinquent behaviour.

Similar observations may be found in the studies of Cockburn and Maclay [41]; Cowie et al. [56]; Adamek and Dager [60]; Cloninger and Guze [61]; Reige [62]; and Richardson [52].

The fourth theme concerns the tendency in criminological theory to associate girls' delinquent or 'difficult' behaviour with mental instability and non-rational behaviour. As we have seen, this is a familiar theme in consideration of women's behaviour. Some of the psychological problems are described in Hoghughi's study of disturbed juvenile delinquents [63]. In *Troubled and Troublesome*, where he reports on the operation of a secure unit of children and young people, he notes that

'. . . . the girls emerge as substantially the more abnormal group in comparison with both extreme and ordinary boys. Fewer girls are seen clinically as impulsive and extroverted with a delinquent self-image but more are emotionally and socially immature, aggressive, deficient in self-control, stubborn and emotionally unstable' [63].

Indeed, it is often assumed that girls in trouble are not sophisticated delinquents but rather deprived and sensitive adolescents.

In summary, we can see that girl delinquents are typically described as 'disturbed', 'undersocialised', 'wayward' and as 'sexual delinquents'. Male offenders, on the other hand, have been described as inherently more criminally inclined and as rational adventurous beings almost to the point of delinquency being seen as a natural part of boys' testing out of the boundaries of masculinity, and as a natural part of their adolescence.

Much of this accumulated wisdom about girls, however, is mythical and misconceived. Official statistics, for example, suggest that many fewer girls than boys commit crimes but we cannot assume that these statistics present an accurate picture. The validity of statistics may be brought into question through notions of bias and omission and importantly, through the findings of self-report studies [64], though these kinds of studies are generally beset with problems (boasting, under-reporting and the like). Also, it is only logical that since most females apparently conform, those who do not are bound to be seen as very different and perhaps as being worse than males. More significantly, if we hold ideas about girls which are more in line with help and treatment we should perhaps look more at agencies *allied* to the criminal justice system – social work agencies, for instance, or psychiatric and adolescent units. Perhaps it is the case that girls' behaviour is defined or interpreted in a different way to boys' behaviour and in a way which leads them into a network of children's homes, assessment centres, secure units and so on rather than into the criminal justice system [65,66,58, c.f.55].

Another point to note is that while people talk of *differences* between girls and boys, this can sometimes lead to a neglect of, or even failure to perceive, *shared* characteristics. So sex differences become exaggerated.

Further, some biological explanations for girls' offending behaviour confuse nature and nurture. Indeed, instead of looking at the combined effects of environmental influences, cultural traditions and physiological, psychological and social factors, biological theorists see criminality solely as the product of hereditary characteristics. Admittedly, this is not a clear-cut distinction. However, many of the characteristics of individuals which have been described as evolutionary have now been shown to be more closely related to social contexts than to any notion of 'naturalness' [46]. Even some physical differences can be explained in social terms, for example, the sexual division of labour. Consider some of the physical descriptions of girls in penal institutions and care homes – 'physically immature, oversized, lumpish and fat . . .', the real questions here are to what extent do such institutions afford girls the opportunity to look any different and are these properties inherent in the girls themselves or are they selected and sustained by the social institutions through which they pass?

Nor do psychological differences between males and females when considered in isolation from other factors, provide an adequate explanation for presumed differences in behaviour. Socialisation clearly plays a part in the development of sexual identity and appropriate sex-role behaviour both by prescription and by implicit expectation. Thus girls are really no more dependent in childhood than boys, girls remain closer to families simply because they are socialised to do this and they are then controlled and supervised in this way. To argue that girls *need* the close affectional ties of the family more than boys, and that they are more disturbed than boys when faced with family disruption and upsets, is not only to deny a variety of experiences amongst both girls and boys, but it is an argument which functions to perpetuate the status quo. It is an argument which can be used to keep girls firmly in their place – at home.

Assumptions about girls' sexual offending also require close attention. While writers and official statistics suggest that girls manifest their disturbances in this way, there is need to question to what extent girls' and boys' behaviour might be 'policed' differently. Research evidence suggests that paternalistic concerns about girls' moral welfare sometimes leads to them being judged not only for what they have done in terms of criminal offences, but for *who* they are and how they behave more generally [38,58].

In contrast, it is largely the case that boys are judged for what they have done. Indeed, assumptions about what a typical girl delinquent is like or needs have sometimes led practitioners, magistrates and judges and Scottish panel hearing members to focus on girls' social and sexual behaviour instead of their offences. In other words, they will ask questions of girls to discover whether or not they stay out late, are disobedient towards parents or promiscuous and these are questions which are not asked of boys.

The point is that there is a double standard in judging girls' and boys' behaviour which is unjust, and where preventive action such as imposing a care order on a girl is taken in the girl's 'best interests', this is not necessarily perceived or experienced as the best action by the girl herself. On the contrary, a 'care order' may be experienced as harsh and punitive. Where the 'pathological perspective' on girls' offending leads to them being dealt with outside the criminal justice system or through care proceedings instead of criminal proceedings, we have to consider whether or not this response is more intrusive or more invidious than direct control through the criminal justice system. One significant point here as I have already stated is that behaviour such as sexual promiscuity, staying out and so on, carry a greater likelihood of removal to institutions than do criminal offences. This is true in both England and Scotland.

IMPLICATIONS FOR PRACTICE

The issues facing practitioners in this sphere are complex and solutions not readily apparent. Nevertheless, all those who have dealings with young people have a part to play in questioning the 'accumulated wisdom' about them. Where early commentators see distinct differences between the behaviour of females and males, practitioners should question whether or not the perception of differences reflects research methodologies rather than actual differences. Where 'essential truths' are proffered, there is need to relate those truths to the social, political and cultural contexts in which they were formed. Where claims are made about distinctive behavioural characteristics of females there is need to question whether or not such claims reflect a focused surveillance and 'policing' of females' activities, leading to an overemphasis on females' sexual and emotional proclivities in analyses of their offending or 'difficult' behaviour.

For those who work in social work, probation work, youth work or intermediate treatment, it is important to consider whether Social Inquiry Reports or other such reports reflect differential concerns about males' and females' behaviour or a differential understanding of it. Preconceptions of what is 'normal' behaviour for males and females may well obscure and distort any clear understanding. The use of stereotypes frequently leads to concentration on certain areas of behaviour at the expense of others, and this must be avoided. For instance, there is a tendency amongst report writers, in their attempt to understand delinquent and difficult behaviour, to concentrate on peer group pressures with regard to boys. With girls, this factor has been largely ignored, with a preference instead for more attention being paid to relationships, particularly within the family. There is a tendency too to provide physical descriptions of girls in reports in a way which would not occur with boys. This different way of looking at the same behaviour, dependent upon the sex of the subject, might lead the report writer to suggest a more serious disposal for a girl than for a boy with similar problems. Clearly, a less serious disposal may well be equally effective in dealing with the girl's problems.

For those who work in residential care the issues relate to whether or not girls prove more difficult to manage and it is important to question why this might be so. To what extent do different expectations of girls' and boys' behaviour influence levels of tolerance, for instance, and how have these levels of tolerance been established? Do they reflect personal socialisation experiences rather than any intrinsic qualities of the youngsters themselves? Indeed, perhaps we emphasise the 'pathological perspective' in relation to girls because we like to see ourselves as counsellors, 'carers', 'older sisters', 'mother' or 'father' figures, for example, and armed with all our images and expectations of girls they have more 'pathological potential' than boys to exploit.

Finally, the issue of whether or not 'equality of treatment' can or even should be created has to be addressed. Some writers and practitioners [67] have argued that to change policy and practice to create a fair system means that girls should be treated like boys. What are the implications of such changes? Would it mean extending the tariff for girls and more girls receiving custodial sentences, for instance, even though custody has no obvious effects in deterring offenders and indeed proves to be a destructive and brutalising experience for many? And which girls would end up in Attendance Centres – those who commit typically 'male offences', those who might be at risk of receiving custodial sentences, or those who presently receive conditional discharges or fines or supervision orders?

The key issue here is once again whether or not 'justice' implies equal treatment or equal provision. There is a danger that equal provision for males and females could result in an escalation up the sentencing tariff for girls since the current tariff in use for them is a shortened version of the one for boys (there are no Detention Centres for girls and few Attendance Centres in the English system). It is conceivable, of course, that desirable change might be to treat boys like girls, to apply to them all the concerns about social and sexual behaviour and to depend more upon a welfare perspective in dealing with their delinquency. But the iniquities of a system like this which allows wide discretion and decision-making are well rehearsed.

Clearly, it is important for practitioners to sort out false perceptions and perspectives. It is also important to sort out the good and bad elements in welfare perspectives or juvenile justice – wide use of discretion should not result in deeds being ignored at the expense of needs, but there should perhaps be a balance between the two, for boys and girls. In so far as juvenile justice systems are always local systems, however, there can be no dictate as to how issues can be resolved, and it is for those involved in such systems to closely monitor changes in policy and practice so that their work is always informed and false perceptions and perspectives held in check.

References

1. Atkins, S. & Hoggett, B. *Women and the Law*. Basil Blackwell, Oxford.

2. Reid, I. & Wormald, E. (Eds.) *Sex Differences in Britain. Grant McIntyre, London, 1982*.

3. Evans, M. & Ungerson, C. (Eds.) *Sexual Divisions: Patterns and Processes*. Tavistock, London, 1983.

4. Gamarnikow, E., Morgan, D., Purvis, J. & Taylorson, D. (Eds.) *The Public and the Private*. Heinemann, London, 1983.

5. Smart, C. *The Ties That Bind. Law, Marriage and the Reproduction of Patriarchal Relations*. Routledge & Kegan Paul, London, 1984.

6. *Critical Social Policy*. Special Feminist Issue. Issue 16, Summer. Longman, Essex, 1986.

7. Hutter, B. & Williams, G. (Eds.) *Controlling Women: The Normal and the Deviant*. Croom Helm in association with the Oxford University Women's Studies Committee, 1981.

8. Datesman, S. & Scarpitti, P., 'Unequal Protection for Males and Females in the Juvenile Court'. In Datesman, S. & Scarpitti, F. (Eds.) *Women, Crime and Justice*. OUP, New York, 1980.

9. Datesman, S. & Scarpitti, F. 'Female Delinquency and Broken Homes: A Reassessment'. In Datesman, S. and Scarpitti, F. (Eds.) *Women, Crime and Justice*, OUP, New York, 1980.

10. De Fleur, L. B. 'Biasing Influences on Drug Arrest Records' *American Sociological Review*, 40, 1975, 88-103.

11. Hudson, B. 'Social Workers and the Discourse of Femininity'. University of Lancaster, Department of Social Administration (unpublished paper), 1981.

12. West, D.J. *The Young Offender*. Penguin, Harmondsworth, 1967

13. West, D.J. & Farrington, D.P. *The Delinquent Way of Life*. Heinemann, London, 1977.

14. Heidensohn, F. 'Sex, Crime and Society'. In Harrison, G.A. & Perl, J. (Eds.) 'Biosocial Aspects of Sex', *Journal of Biosocial Science Supplement*. 2, May, 1970.

15. Criminal Law Revision Committee, *Prostitution in the Street*. 16th Report, HMSO, London, 1984.

16. Hindelang, M.J. 'Sex Differences in Criminal Activity' *Social Problems*. 27, 1979, 143-156.

17. Cameron, M.O. *The Booster and the Snitch: Department Store Shoplifting*. Collier-Macmillan, Glencoe, 1964.

18. Hindelang, M.J. 'Decisions of Shoplifting Victims to Invoke the Criminal Justice Process' *Social Problems*. 21, 1974, 580-593.

19. Box, S. *Power, Crime and Mystification*. Tavistock, London, 1983.

20. Piliavin, I. & Briar, S. 'Police Encounters with Juveniles' *American Journal of Sociology*. 70, 1964, 206-214.

21. Black, D.J. & Reiss, A.J. 'Police Control of Juveniles' *American Journal of Sociology*. 75, 1970, 63-77.

22. Mawby, R.I. 'Sex and Crime: The Results of a Self-Report Study' *British Journal of Sociology*. 31, 4, 1980, 525-545.

23. Carey, K. 'Police Policy and the Prosecution of Women'. Paper presented to British Sociological Association conference (unpublished), 1979.

24. Rettig, S. & Pasamanick, B. 'Differences in the Structures of Moral Values of Students and Alumni' *American Sociological Review*. 25, 4, 1960, 550-555.

25. Chesney Lind, M. 'Judicial Enforcement of the Female Sex Role: The Family Court, and the Female Delinquent' *Issues in Criminology*. 8, 1973, 51-69.

26. Terry, R.M. 'Discrimination in the Handling of Juvenile Offenders by Social Control Agencies'. In Garabedian, P.G. & Gibbons, D.C. (Eds.) *Becoming Delinquent*. Aldine Press, New York, 1970.

27. Visher, C.A. 'Gender, Police Arrest Decisions, and Notions of Chivalry' *Criminology*. 21, 1, 1983, 5-28.

28. Nagel, I. 'Sex Differences in the Processing of Criminal Defendants'. In Morris, A.M. & Gelsthorpe, L.R. (Eds.) *Women and Crime*. Cropwood Conferences Series No.13, Institute of Criminology, University of Cambridge, 1981.

29. Farrington, D.P. & Morris, A.M. 'Do Magistrates Discriminate Against Men?' *Justice of the Peace*. Sept 17th, 1983, 601-603.

30. Thomas, D.A. *Principles of Sentencing*. Heinemann, London (second edition), 1979.

31. Eaton, M. 'Mitigating Circumstances: Familiar Rhetoric' *International Journal of the Sociology of Law*. 11, 4, 1983, 385-400.

32. Carlen, P. *Women's Imprisonment. Routledge & Kegan Paul, London, 1983.*

33. *Pearson, R. 'Women Defendants in Magistrates' Courts' British Journal of Law and Society.* 3, 1976, 265-273.

34. Edwards, S. *Women on Trial*. Manchester University Press, Manchester, 1984.

35. Sarri, R. & Hasenfeld, Y. *Brought to Justice: Juveniles, the Courts and the Law*. National Assessment of Juvenile Corrections, University of Michigan, Ann Arbor, 1976.

36. Armstrong, G. 'Females Under the Law Protected but Unequal' Crime and Delinquency. 23, 2, 1977, 109-120.

37. Casburn, M. *Girls Will Be Girls: Sexism and Juvenile Justice in a London Borough*. Women's Research and Resources Centre Publications, London, 1979.

38. Gelsthorpe, L.R. *Girls, Crime and Justice*. (Audio-tape), Information Systems, Lancaster, 1985.

39. Warren, J. 'Juvenile Justice in Scotland and England: How Boys and Girls Fare'. Paper given to conference on the Prevention and Treatment of Juvenile Delinquency Among

Girls in the EEC, European University Institute, Florence, 1985.

40. Simon, R.J. *Women and Crime*. D.C. Heath & Co., Lexington, Mass., 1975.

41. Cockburn, J.J. & Maclay, I. 'Sex Differences in Juvenile Delinquency' *British Journal of Criminology*. 5, 3, 1965, 289-303.

42. May, D. 'Delinquent Girls Before the Courts' *Medicine, Science and the Law*. 17, 1977, 202-212.

43. Wadsworth, M. *Roots of Delinquency: Infancy, Adolescence and Crime*. Martin Robertson, Oxford, 1979.

44. Worrall, A. 'Out of Place: Female Offenders in the Coiurt' *Probation Journal*. 28, 1981, 90-93.

45. Dominelli, L. 'Differential Justice: Domestic Labour, Community Service and Female Offenders' *Probation Journal*. 31, 1984, 100-103.

46. Morris, A.M. & Gelsthorpe, L.R. 'False Clues and Female Crime'. In Morris, A.M. & Gelsthorpe, L.R. (Eds.) *Women and Crime*. Cropwood Conference Series No. 13, Institute of Criminology, University of Cambridge, 1981.

47. Heidensohn, F. *Women and Crime*. Macmillan, London, 1985. (See especially chapter 4 – Women and the Penal System).

48. Gelsthorpe, L.R. 'Girls and Their Treatment in the Criminal Juvenile Justice System' (forthcoming, 1987).

49. Carpenter, M. *Juvenile Delinquents. Social Evils, Their Causes and Their Cure*. Cash, London, 1853.

50. Morris, A.M. with McIsaac, M. *Juvenile Justice?*. Heinemann, London, 1978.

51. Association of Headmasters, Headmistresses and Matrons of Approved Schools. (Technical Sub-Committee) *Girls in Approved Schools*. Monograph no.6, issued as supplement to the Approved Schools Gazette no.48 (April) 1954.

52. Ball, J.C. & Logan, N. 'Early Sexual Behaviour of Lower Class Delinquent Girls' *Journal of Criminal Law, Criminology and Police Science*. 51, 1960, 208-214. Richardson, H.J. *Adolescent Girls in Approved Schools*. Routledge & Kegan Paul, London, 1969.

53. Walker, A. 'Special Problems of Delinquent and Maladjusted Girls' *Approved Schools Gazette*. 55, 7, 1961, 270-278.

54. Home Office Advisory Council on the Penal System. Detention of Girls in the Detention Centre. *Interim Report*. HMSO, London, 1968.

55. Rutter, M. & Giller, H. *Juvenile Delinquency Trends and Perspectives*. Penguin, Harmondsworth, Middlesex, 1983.

56. Cowie, J., Cowie, V. & Slater, E. *Delinquency in Girls*. Heinemann, London, 1968, 167.

57. Shaklady Smith, L. 'Sexist Assumptions and Female Delinquency. An Empirical Investigation'. In Smart, C. & Smart, B. (Eds.) *Women, Sexuality and Social Control*. Routledge & Kegan Paul, London, 1976.

58. Campbell, A. *Girl Delinquents*. Basil Blackwell, Oxford, 1981.

59. Morris, R. 'Female Delinquents and Relational Problems' *Social Forces*. 43, 1964, 82-89.

60. Adamek, R.J. & Dager, E.Z. 'Familial Experience, Identification and Female Delinquency' *Sociological Focus*. 2, spring 1969, 37-62.

61. Cloninger, C.R. & Guze, S.B. 'Female Criminals: Their Personal, Familial and Social Backgrounds' *Archives of General Psychiatry*. 23 (December 1970), 554-558.

62. Reige, M.G. 'Parental Affection and Juvenile Delinquency in Girls' *British Journal of Criminology*. 12, 1, 1972, 55-73.

63. Hoghughi, M. *Troubled and Troublesome: Coping with Severely Disordered Children*. Burnett, London, 1978.

64. Box, S. *Deviance, Reality and Society*. Holt, Rinehart and Winston, London, 1981 (2nd edition). (See chapters 1 & 3).

65. Procek, E. 'Psychiatry and the Social Control of Women'. In Morris, A.M. & Gelsthorpe, L.R. (Eds.) *Women and Crime*. Cropwood Conference Series No.13, Institute of Criminology, University of Cambridge, 1981.

66. Caplan, P.J., Awad, G.H., Wilks, C. & White, G. 'Sex Differences in a Delinquent Clinic Population' *British Journal of Criminology*. 20, 1980, 311-328.

67. Johnson, N.H. 'Special Problems of the Female Offender' *Juvenile Justice*. 28, 3, 1977, 3-10.

The Gender of the Therapist: Its Relevance to Practice and Training

Elizabeth Hall

This chapter considers the research into the influence of the gender of the worker in therapeutic relationships. It uses the literature of psychotherapy to highlight issues of relevance to all worker-client relationships, but especially where the exploration and understanding of emotional difficulties are involved. However, the influence of gender and sex-role stereotyping remain important even when the worker-client interaction focusses on practical issues, for example, housing and employment.

THERAPIST GENDER: Empirical Research

The importance of the gender of the therapist in psychotherapy/counselling has usually been examined by the study of a few experimental variables and their relationship to the gender of the therapist or client. The empirical research presents a confusing and often contradictory picture of the relevance of gender to the therapeutic encounter. There are few studies of actual therapy and most studies use an analogue methodology with its limitations of stimulus material (brief vignettes, case descriptions or video-taped role-plays) and number of variables studied. It does not incorporate the range of verbal and non-verbal interaction that is an integral part of the therapeutic process. Analogue research may, however, be most valuable in gaining preliminary information that can be verified in naturalistic studies [1].

Reviews have concluded that the gender of therapist is not a critical factor in the outcome of therapy [2,3]. This conclusion has been drawn after analysis of large numbers of widely differing, but mainly analogue, studies. Smith [3] subjected these studies to a meta-analysis and found no therapist gender effect. But no account was taken of the *differences* between the studies. For instance, the training and experience of therapists varied, and the studies used problems ranging from strictly vocational issues to severe emotional difficulties. Furthermore, some of the research quoted used college students who were not even seeking therapy as subjects. It is likely that these methodological differences may have reduced the chance of detecting a gender effect.

With studies using qualified therapists/counsellors, genuine clients and mainly emotional difficulties as their problem area, a different picture emerges however. It has been found that therapists behave in ways consistent with sex-role expectations. Male therapists have been shown to expect to be more directive than their female colleagues [4]. Furthermore, female counsellors have rated themselves as more empathic [5,6] and more able to accept the client's attributions about the cause of his/her difficulties [7] than male counsellors. Johnson [5] also found that although her female counsellors had angry feelings about the client, they were more able to maintain their empathic responses to the client.

An analogue study by Billingsley [8] suggests that therapists may have become more aware of the limitations of some of the sex-role expectations. *Male* therapists were shown to choose significantly more *feminine* treatment goals (e.g. expression of feelings) whereas *female* therapists chose more *masculine* goals (e.g. greater assertiveness and activity) for all clients. This was confirmed by Murray and Abramson [9] who found that female therapists stressed the need for work on assertiveness more often and sooner than male therapists.

It is likely that therapist attitudes and information about men and women will influence any therapeutic contact. It has been shown that *both* male and female therapists exhibit stereotyped attitudes about men and women [10,11]. It is usually assumed that such attitudes and roles must hinder and never facilitate therapy. Since 'male' characteristics are more likely to be more highly valued than 'female' characteristics [12], the consequences of stereotyping are mostly discussed in relation to women.

In a survey of *female* psychologists [10], the following areas of stereotyping affecting women as clients emerged:

(1) fostering traditional sex roles
(2) bias in expectations and devaluation of women
(3) responding to women as sex objects, including seduction of female clients by male therapists
(4) sexist use of psychoanalytic concepts.

This survey surprisingly excluded male psychologists, and issues affecting men as clients (e.g. adjustment to changes in the traditional fathering role, primacy of work and the discouragement of the expression of feelings).

In spite of a number of methodological criticisms [2,13], a study by Broverman et al. [11] continues to be the most quoted research demonstrating the existence of stereotyped attitudes of the therapist. Clinicians were asked to rate either a 'healthy adult male', a 'healthy adult female' or a 'healthy adult' on the sex-role stereotype questionnaire [12]. There was no difference between the ratings of male and female clinicians, but strong agreement on the behaviour and attributes characterising a healthy man, a woman and adult respectively. The healthy woman was rated as being *less* healthy than the healthy adult, whereas the ratings of the healthy adult and the healthy male did not differ. Later studies confirmed these findings but for *male* therapists only [3,14,15].

In a study of therapist attitudes and information about women, Sherman et al. [16] found that female therapists held better informed, more liberal, and less stereotyped views than male therapists. Male therapists were, however, over-represented by a factor of 2:1 and this may have influenced the results. The evidence, therefore, indicates that therapists – both *male and female* – are affected by the prevailing sex-role stereotypes about men and women. There is some suggestion that male therapists are more bound to the traditional expectations about women than female therapists, but studies have not examined the traditional expectations about men. It is possible that similar stereotypes about the male role exist. There is cause for concern that therapists may not be as well-informed about gender-related issues as might be hoped [16,17].

Interaction Between Client and Therapist Gender

The feminist movement has stressed that women clients should be seen by female therapists, because only women can really understand women. Research on the sex-pairings of clients and therapists is often confusing and contradictory.

Early work on client preferences for a therapist of one gender rather than the other, suggested that those clients who stated a preference on entering therapy usually preferred a male to a female therapist [18]. More recently, at least for college students seeking counselling, this had changed [19]. Over 90 per cent of the female students preferred to have a female therapist, whereas the male students were evenly divided in their preference for male or female therapist. It is likely that this reflects a change in the prevailing social attitudes as well as an awareness of the increased availability of female therapists.

The length of therapy has also been highlighted as a problem for *female* clients who were said to be 'kept' in therapy longer by their male therapist [18]. It has been shown that women tend to remain in therapy longer than men [20] but more detailed research has shown that patients paired with same-sex therapists tend to remain in therapy longer than patients in a mixed-sex pairing [21,22].

The return of clients to therapy after the initial session has been shown to vary with the gender of the counsellor [23,24,25], but no consistent picture emerges with both male [25] and female [23,24] counsellors reducing the return rate.

Evidence from studies examining the process of therapy has shown that greater satisfaction has been reported by female clients after therapy sessions with female therapists than with male therapists [26], especially for single women aged 23-28 [27]. Furthermore, Hill [28] found that same-sex pairing facilitated the disclosure of feelings. She noted an effect of the experience of the counsellor. With female clients, *experienced female* counsellors were more empathic, satisfied and involved, and with male clients, more facilitative and active than inexperienced female counsellors. The same was not true for the *male* counsellors, where the *inexperienced* counsellors were more empathic and active with clients of both sexes. The female counsellor's experience tended to make her react in a way that was consistent with the sex-role of her clients.

Orlinsky and Howard [27] found that many of their female clients paired with male therapists reported less comfort and support, more involvement and self-criticalness but not necessarily less benefit from their therapy. Furthermore, their younger single women (18-22 years), in therapy with male therapists, reported a more intense desire for active input from the therapist, greater concern with identity, fear and anger, feelings of great inhibition, less self-possession and open-ness and a view of the therapist as more detached and demanding.

Finally, in one area of research, agreement does seem better – namely the area of sexuality, including physical attractiveness and sexual contact between patients and therapists [29,30,31]. Historically Freud [32] saw the sexual reactions of the client as part of the 'transference' that had to be worked through. Analysts were exhorted to renounce all erotic feelings for the patient, as they were seen as a hindrance to successful analysis. Schover [31] stresses that this ignores human nature and psychoanalysts have gradually recognised that acknowledgement of these feelings is more useful.

It has been noted that the attractiveness of patients can affect psychotherapists' judgements quite significantly [9]. Although physical attractiveness has been neglected in psychotherapy research, the psychological literature indicates that attractiveness is a powerful determinant of the course of social interaction [33]. Bar-Tal and Saxe [34] concluded that attractiveness is more important in the evaluation of females than in males. Murray and Abramson [9] conclude their review by suggesting that

> 'therapists take a more positive view of attractive clients especially in the case of women, and prefer to work with clients who are attractive.'

Client attractiveness appears to affect a number of process variables in psychotherapy. Perlmutter [30] interviewed mainly male therapists and found that most difficulties reported were with 'beautiful' female clients. He found that working with attractive female clients led to uncertainty about goals of therapy and diagnosis. Intrapsychic interpretations were used even when there was evidence to the contrary (e.g. physical abuse by the client's spouse). Furthermore, verbal psychotherapy was used more often with the attractive female client even when the therapist usually used behavioural approaches.

It has been stated that sexual feelings between therapist and client are an integral part of any therapeutic interaction [35]. Scheflen's [36] work on 'quasi-courtship' behaviour during therapy has concluded that as long as therapists and clients distinguish 'quasi-courtship' from real courtship, it can be a positive force in therapy.

It has been consistently shown that it is the male therapist who has sexual feelings or actual contact with attractive female clients [29]. In an extensive analogue study of the effect of client gender, seductiveness and sexual material on therapists' verbal responses, emotional reactions and clinical judgements, Schover [31] found that male therapists had erotic responses to female clients especially if the client was attractive. The therapists then verbally encouraged the client to discuss their sexual experiences. A number revealed sexual feelings for the client although recognising the limits on sexual behaviour in therapy, whilst others, especially those who had conservative attitudes towards issues of sexuality, spoke of their anxiety, anger and disapproval towards the seductive client.

On the other hand, female therapists reported very little sexual arousal, and did not feel a need to share their feelings with the seductive male client. They appeared to show neither voyeuristic nor avoidance responses. Schover suggests they may need help in asserting limits with seductive clients and in focussing on hostile or resistive aspects of such interactions. Furthermore, they may fear for their safety, but may also be more practised at avoiding seductiveness in men.

It can be seen, therefore, that when psychotherapists ignore the issue of sexuality in themselves and their clients, difficulties can arise in therapy. As far as actual sexual contact between therapist and client (usually male therapist – female client) is concerned, Holroyd concludes that

> 'patient-therapist sex occurs when therapists who have mental and emotional problems also have sexist values.'

From this review, it can be seen that far from having no effect as concluded by Smith [3] and Whitely [2], therapist gender is an important factor in a number of ways. Both process and outcome research has indicated that gender cannot be ignored as a significant influence in psychotherapy and counselling.

ASPECTS OF THE THERAPEUTIC RELATIONSHIP

It has been argued that the 'sex bias paradigm' of the empirical research is too superficial and produces too many contradictions [38]. It ignores too many variables, e.g. problem and therapy types, setting and expectations of therapy, severity of problems, age of client and therapist, quite apart from the interactional variables that operate within the therapeutic session.

Davidson [38] argues that the concept of counter-transference may be useful in moving the research to a more fruitful and in-depth investigation of the contribution of therapist gender. She stresses the need to combine the purely classical definition of counter-transference relating to unconscious conflicts within the therapist with the use of therapist reactions as a data source [39] about the process of therapy. More specifically, this reconceptualisation allows examination of both the personal history and interpersonal dynamics on one hand, and the cognitive, behavioural and emotional processes of the therapist on the other. Clearly, this view would accept that therapists are products of their socialisation as male or female.

A classification of counter-transference by Lakovics [40] usefully extends Davidson's reconceptualisation of sex bias in that it helps to clarify the facilitating and inhibiting aspects of therapist responses. Five of his six types of counter-transference response seem to have particular relevance to the examination of gender-related reactions in the therapist:

1) *'Concordant Identification'* is an empathic response that occurs when the therapist's reactions mirror those of the client. Clearly, concordant identification of gender-related reactions should occur more frequently in same-sex therapist-client pairings.

2) *'Complementary Identification'* occurs when the therapist identifies with the client's significant 'internal objects', e.g. parents. Thus, issues of parenting with their gender-loaded implications are likely to be apparent.

3) The *'Interactional Reactions'* are the conscious responses of the therapist to the client's behaviour in the therapy session. This clearly includes communication patterns in their widest sense including verbal and non-verbal behaviour, appearance and clothing. It has been shown that personal space needs and interactional styles are different for the sexes [41]. For example, women tolerate and prefer reduced distances between themselves and others [42], are more sensitive to their own and others' non-verbal behaviour than men [43] and engage in more eye contact than men [44]. Furthermore, styles of interaction (e.g. competitive, conforming styles) are likely to be different for the sexes. The therapist who uses the behaviour appropriate for his or her gender may be more readily accepted by the client than one who uses gender-inappropriate behaviour, and this may be important at the early stages of establishing a therapeutic relationship.

4) *'Life Events'* of the therapist can provide a useful source of information where they are gender-specific, e.g. the effects of gynaecological and other physical (e.g. mastectomy, vasectomy, childbirth etc.) procedures.

5) *Classical Counter-transference* which relates to unconscious feelings and impulses toward the client which result from the therapist's past conflicts. There may be resistances and defences that are gender-specific, e.g. issues of emotional expression, dependency and sexuality.

One final area of therapist reactions to the client, omitted from Lakovics' classification, is that of *therapist identification* with the client because of similarities between the client's and therapist's life experiences. These may not be an area of unconscious conflict and resistance, but may represent useful experiences which could facilitate the client's therapy. This kind of facilitation is a very significant part of the self-help group ethos where individuals who have worked through a particular difficulty, counsel others who are experiencing similar problems. Thus, there may be positive advantages in pairing therapist and client together where some of the therapist's life experiences are similar (and are not a source of conflict) to the problems of the client. Goz [45], for instance, found that her personal experiences during pregnancy (which actually occurred during the client's therapy) were a distinct advantage in the successful therapeutic outcome with an expectant mother.

Davidson's reconceptualisation of sex bias in counter-transference terms, and Lakovics' classification of counter-transference would therefore seem to add considerably to the understanding of the mediation of gender-related influences in and on the therapeutic relationship, but is most informative for the *individual* therapist. There are general features of sex-role learning that have relevance and will be discussed separately.

THE SEX-ROLE OF THE THERAPIST

Certain features of the sex-role expectations seem particularly relevant to the examination of the influence of gender in the therapist: namely, the expression and use of emotional feelings; competence, achievement and success; power; the importance of relationships, and sexuality.

1. Expression and use of Emotional Feelings

The expression of and sensitivity to emotional feelings are part of the sex-role expectations for both males and females. Expression of warmth and empathy is discouraged for males and encouraged for females. The opposite is true for anger. It is suggested that male therapists may have only a cognitive awareness of the feelings of others and not the 'vicarious' responses of the female therapist [46]. The female therapist may, however, be less able to be emotionally detached because of her sex-role prescription of greater emotional involvement. The female therapist would, therefore, be out of her sex-role by maintaining some emotional distance, and the male therapist would be out of his by being empathic. Whilst the therapist may have resolved these conflicts, the clients may be confused by such behaviour.

Furthermore, expression of distress and acceptance of the distress of others is considered more in keeping with the female role. Thus, therapists may be more comfortable with the distress of their female clients. In addition, clients are probably more likely to show distress to a female therapist. In a male-male pairing, client distress may be inhibited for fear of appearing weak or unmasculine.

Expression and acknowledgement of anger in therapy may be particularly difficult for female therapists and clients since females are socialised to restrict their expression of anger to such an extent that even its aknowledgement can be difficult. It has been concluded that women gain valuable sources of self-esteem from their relationships [47,48,49] and that they act to maintain and enhance these relationship ties. Anger and its expression threatens this maintenance of relationships. Thus, the female therapist is likely to deny anger in herself and become emotionally distant when she suppresses her anger consciously [49]. Furthermore, she is more likely to use oblique or covert forms of anger [50] than her male counterpart.

Thus, there are many aspects of emotional expression that have different consequences for male and female therapists. These consequences are subtle and the nature of their manifestation will depend on the individual therapist and client.

2. *Competence, Achievement and Success*

These areas are usually seen as part of the male sex-role, although recent cultural changes accepting women at work have brought these issues into focus.

It has been suggested that women have a fear of *success* whereas men have a fear of *failure* [51]. Therapists, therefore, may react differently to success and failure both in themselves and their clients. Furthermore, women tend to assign success to luck rather than to their own competence [51]. The female therapist who makes this assumption about success in therapy, will be less able to capitalise on the positive and facilitating aspects of her performance.

Competitiveness is often associated with the male role to such an extent that women are likely to deny their competitiveness. Female therapists, in particular, need to be aware of its existence in themselves and their clients in order to prevent difficulties in therapy.

3. *Power/Authority*

Psychotherapy involves an unequal relationship – the therapist is seen to be an expert in providing the solutions to psychological difficulties, on which the client is dependent. Traditionally, men are seen as being more powerful than women. The female therapist may have more difficulties in using the power and authority consistent with her role as therapist, because of the strong socialisation pressures to be seen as less powerful in relationships.

It is likely that since women are not usually recognised as authority figures, the competence and authority of a female therapist may be questioned more often [52]. The female therapist, on her part, should be particularly attentive to behaviour that undermines her authority (e.g. indecisiveness, willingness to relax the boundaries of the therapeutic hour, and the submissive or low status non-verbal cues of discomfort with eye contact, too frequent smiling, over-anxiety and too casual dress).

4. *The Importance of Relationships*

Women are thought more likely to use their relationships as a source of self-esteem [48]. Therefore, the female therapist may find it harder to deal with termination of therapy, and may be more personally threatened by a client terminating early. This has been partially confirmed by Greene [53] who showed that female social workers became more anxious and emotionally closer to their clients at termination. Male therapists, by contrast, became more emotionally impassive and distant.

5. *Sexuality*

The sex-role prescriptions of sexuality are very different for the sexes – the female is expected to appear attractive and to inhibit her overt sexuality. The male's sexual responses are seen as more acceptable and natural. For the male therapist, the problems seem to be most acute when faced with an attractive female client [31]. For the female therapist, the difficulties are more likely to be a result of denial or inhibition of sexual responses, particularly with male patients.

Finally, all therapists need to be aware that their attractiveness will affect male and female clients differently. This is likely to be most obvious in opposite-sex pairings, but should not be ignored in same-sex pairings.

CONCLUSIONS

It can be seen from the foregoing discussion that the gender of the therapist is likely to play an important role in the process, and possibly the outcome, of psychotherapy. It is suggested that a reconceptualisation of the sex-bias paradigm of the empirical research is long overdue, and a careful analysis of the relevance of the gender of both therapist and client be undertaken to examine the subtleties of the therapeutic interaction. The search for bias

B. Discussion

against one sex or the other has ignored the fact that gender is an important factor in social interaction processes, and there seems no reason to assume that therapeutic interaction should be free from such influence just because it occurs behind the doors of the consulting room.

The conclusion has immediate implications for the training of therapists and for the choice of the gender of the therapist for particular clients. The following recommendations for training are suggested: *Discussion.*

1. Training schemes should incorporate gender-related issues in their widest sense. This should include the physical (e.g. menstruation, contraception, childbirth etc.) and psychological aspects (e.g. work, marriage, child-rearing) of being male and female. Much of the recent literature has stressed the importance of this kind of training in women's issues but this creates a new kind of sexism, i.e. ignoring similar issues for men.

2. Training should involve an understanding of how society's pressures and demands affect men and women differently. These issues are as relevant as an understanding of intrapsychic processes.

3. Training with both male and female supervisors is important, but should be used more constructively to include an examination of gender-related issues in therapy. The use of Lakovics' [40] classification of counter-transference and an understanding of the life experiences and problems of the therapist that are gender-specific may facilitate exploration of similar situations with the client.

4. Therapist learning should not stop at the end of formal training, but should continue with mixed-sex groups of colleagues. This is a particularly important part of therapist learning since with increased confidence and self-awareness the therapist may be able to tackle some of the very complex gender-related issues more easily.

5. An important part of training should be increasing an awareness of sexism by omission [54]. Sexism is often dismissed as indicating bad therapy, but therapists may *omit* to ask the relevant questions or to follow up issues raised by the patient, e.g. vocational decisions in women, issues relating to sexuality and alcoholism and difficulties relating to child-rearing.

6. Since gender-mediated influences in therapy may often be at a non-verbal level, a closer scrutiny of communication patterns, both verbal and non-verbal, should be undertaken during training with the use of videotape technology.

Choice of Gender of Therapist

This matter is frequently ignored in the allocation of therapists to patients, and may well be an important issue in establishing a working relationship with a particular patient. Work from voluntary agencies dealing with women has suggested that cases of rape, incest and marital violence against women may be more appropriately dealt with by female therapists [55]. Initially the clients may be too frightened and threatened by men in general to discuss these issues with a male therapist. However, if this early stage of therapy can be passed successfully, the female client may gain more from a male therapist who provides a different model from the abusing male who has been part of her problems.

The choice of therapist on the basis of gender may be important for patients with particular sets of problems, for example, homosexuality [45], or the consequences of inadequate mothering [56]. Carter [56] stresses that in cases where there has been inadequate or absent mothering, a female therapist is more appropriate since the client needs to be able to place the therapist in the maternal role. This may be important especially at the beginning of therapy where the establishment of a working alliance is important for the development of a positive therapeutic relationship. It also seems likely that different problems will be raised, or raised in a different order with therapists of different sexes [57].

The chapter has examined some of the more subtle ways that sex-role expectations and socialisation pressures may influence the therapist. It has indicated that analysis using the gender of therapist and client alone without looking at individual differences in adoption of cultural expectations can lead to erroneous or inadequate conclusions. The question of whether male and female therapists treat their clients differently should start from the premise that all interpersonal relationships are influenced by the gender of the individuals in many different ways. It is likely that increased use of modern technology in recording and analysing the process of therapy will lead to a more accurate assessment of how male and female therapists interact with their clients.

Furthermore, the *facilitatory* aspects of the therapist's sex-role behaviour should be acknowledged. Much of the literature has been examined in terms of bias against one sex or the other and completely ignores the positive aspects of being male or female in our society.

This discussion has suggested that the effects of gender on the therapist and on the process of therapy are widespread, subtle and, as yet, unexplored. It is clear that the frequent criticism of bias against the female client should be re-examined to analyse sources of error, bias and misinterpretation for both male and female clients. It would be a retrograde step to create a new kind of sexism by ignoring similar problems for male clients.

As long as therapists continue to emphasise adjustment to the male or female role as a goal in therapy without looking at individual needs, there will be difficulties. It is time to question clients' expressed satisfaction with traditional roles since an understanding of the meaning of these roles for the *individual* may help clients to change and become more satisfied with their lives in a more realistic way. It is, however, not sufficient to set goals in therapy that involve liberating the client from the sex-role expectations if the client relies on them to support a shaky gender identity. Careful examination of the function and meaning of the sex-role expectations for the client should be undertaken before concluding that these sex-roles are necessarily bad. They may be bad for the therapist but necessary for the client.

Traditional stereotypes still abound in society in spite of some moves towards androgyny [58]. These stereotypes have positive and negative consequences for both sexes. The feminist movement has increased the awareness of some of the biases against women and established a standard of equality of opportunity particularly at work. However, the blurring of boundaries between the roles played by the sexes had led to a number of new problems of adjustment – for women by attempting to combine family and work, for women who wish to continue in the traditional role of mother and homemaker, and for men in the workplace competing and dealing with female colleagues and at home in taking part in the traditionally female activities of child-rearing and home-making.

In the future, therapists are more likely to have to cope with clients who are attempting to adopt non-traditional sex-roles. It is important to be aware of the institutional and social constraints against such non-traditional beha- viour. Until recently this has been the case more with female than with male clients, but any lasting change in the roles of one sex will eventually necessitate a change in the roles of the other. Therapists have an obligation to become aware of these changes and their feelings about them, as well as increasing their appreciation of how they operate as gendered individuals in psychotherapy.

48

References

1. Maracek, J. & Johnson, M. 'Gender and the Process of Psychotherapy'. In Brodsky, A.M. & Hare-Mustin, R.T. (Eds.) *Women and Psychotherapy.* Guildford Press, New York, 1980.

2. Whitely, B.E. 'Sex Roles and Psychotherapy: a Current Appraisal' *Psychological Bulletin.* 86, 1979, 1309-1321.

3. Smith, M.L. 'Sex Bias in Counseling and Psychotherapy' *Psychological Bulletin.* 87, 1980, 392-407.

4. Bernstein, B.L. & Lecomte, K. 'Therapist Expectancies: Client Gender and Therapist Gender, Profession and Level of Training' *Journal of Counseling Psychology.* 36, 1982, 744-754.

5. Johnson, M. 'Influence of Counselor Gender on Reactivity to Clients' *Journal of Counseling Psychology.* 25, 1978, 359-365.

6. Hill, C.E., Tanney, M.F., Leonard, M.M. & Reiss, J.A. 'Counselor Reactions to Female Clients: Types of Problems, Age of Client and Sex of Counselor' *Journal of Counseling Psychology.* 24, 1977, 60-65.

7. Compas, B.E. & Adelman, H.S. 'Clinicians' Judgements of Female Clients' Causal Attributions' *Journal of Clinical Psychology.* 37, 1981, 456-460.

8. Billingsley, D. 'Sex Bias in Psychotherapy: An Examination of the Effects of Client Sex, Client Pathology, and Therapist Sex on Treatment Planning' *Journal of Consulting and Clinical Psychology.* 45, 1977, 250-256.

9. Murray, J. & Abramson, P.R. 'An Investigation of the Effects of Client Gender and Attractiveness on Psychotherapists' Judgments'. In Murray, J. & Abramson, P.R. (Eds.) *Bias in Psychotherapy.* Praeger, New York, 1981.

10. Brodsky, A. & Holroyd, J. *Report of the Task Force on Sex Bias and Sex-Role Stereotyping in Psychotherapeutic Practice.* American Psychological Association, Washington D.C., 1975.

11. Broverman, I.K., Broverman, D.M., Clarkson, F.E., Rosencrantz, P.S. & Vogel, S.R. 'Sex Role Stereotypes and Clinical Judgments of Mental Health' *Journal of Consulting and Clinical Psychology.* 34, 1970, 1-7.

12. Rosencrantz, P.S., Vogel, S.R., Bee, H., Broverman, I.K. & Broverman, D.M. 'Sex Role Stereotypes and Self-Concepts in College Students' *Journal of Consulting and Clinical Psychology.* 32, 1968, 287-295.

13. Stricker, G. 'Implications of Research for Psychotherapeutic Treatment of Women' *American Psychologist.* 32, 1977, 14-22.

14. Aslin, A.L. 'Feminist and Community Mental Health Center Psychotherapists' Expectations of Mental Health for Women' *Sex Roles.* 3, 1977, 537-544.

15. Delk, J.L. & Ryan, T.T. 'A-B Status and Sex Stereotyping Among Psychotherapists and Patients' *Journal of Nervous and Mental Diseases.* 164, 1977, 253-262.

16. Sherman, J.A., Konfacos, C. & Kenworthy, J.A. 'Therapists: Their Attitudes and Information about Women' *Psychology of Women Quarterly.* 2, 1978, 299-313.

17. Hall, E.H. *The Influence of Gender on the Psychotherapist.* Unpublished dissertation, University of Aberdeen, 1985.

18. Chesler, P. *Women and Madness*. Doubleday, New York, 1972.

19. Walker, E. & Stake, J. 'Changes in Preference for Male and Female Counselors' *Journal of Consulting and Clinical Psychology*. 46, 1978, 1153-1154.

20. Abramowitz, S.I., Roback, H.B., Schwartz, J.M., Yasuna, A., Abramowitz, C.V. & Gomes, B. 'Sex Bias in Psychotherapy. A Failure to Confirm' *American Journal of Psychiatry*. *133, 1976, 706-709.*

21. Helms, J.E. 'Counselor Reactions to Female Clients: Generalising from Analogue Research to Counseling Setting' *Journal of Counseling Psychology*. 25, 1978, 193-199.

22. Safer, J. 'Effects of Sex of Patient and Therapist on Length of Therapy' *International Mental Health Research Newsletter*. 12-13, 1973.

23. Epperson, D.L. 'Counselor Gender and Early Premature Terminations from Counseling: A Replication and Extension' *Journal of Counseling Psychology*. 28, 1981, 349-356.

24. Epperson, D.L., Bushway, D.J. & Warman, R.E. 'Client Self-Termination After One Counseling Session – Effects of Problem Recognition, Counselor Gender and Counselor Experience' *Journal of Counseling Psychology*. 30, 1983, 307-315.

25. Shullman, S.L. & Betz, N.E. 'An Investigation of the Effects of Client Sex and Presenting Problem in Referral from Intake' *Journal of Counseling Psychology*. 26, 1979, 140-145.

26. Howard, K.I., Orlinsky, D.W. & Hill, J.A. 'Patients' Satisfaction in Psychotherapy as a Function of Patient-Therapist Pairing' *Psychotherapy, Theory, Research and Practice*. 7, 1970, 130-134.

27. Orlinsky, D.E. & Howard, K.I. 'The Effects of Sex of Therapist on the Therapeutic Experiences of Women' *Psychotherapy, Theory, Research and Practice*. 13, 1976. 82-88.

28. Hill, C.E. 'Sex of Client and Sex and Experience Level of Counselor' *Journal of Counseling Psychology*. 22, 1975, 6-11.

29. Holroyd, J.C. 'Erotic Contact as an Instance of Sex-Biased Therapy'. In Murray, J. & Abramson, P.R. (Eds.) *Bias in Psychotherapy*. Praeger, New York, 1983.

30. Perlmutter, M.S. Study reported in Hatfield, E. & Perlmutter, M.S. 'Social-psychological Issues in Bias: Physical Attractiveness'. In Murray, J. & Abramson, P.R. (Eds.) *Bias in Psychotherapy*. Praeger, New York, 1983.

31. Schover, L.R. 'Psychotherapists' Responses to Client Sexuality: A Source of Bias in Treatment?'. In Murray, J. & Abramson, P.R. (Eds.) *Bias in Psychotherapy*. Praeger, New York, 1983.

32. Freud, S. 'Further Recommendations on the Technique of Psychoanalysis: Observations on Transference Love'. In Strachey J. (Ed.) *Collected Papers*. Vol.2, Hogarth Press, London, 1949.

33. Hatfield, E. & Perlmutter, M.S. 'Social-psychological Issues in Bias: Physical Attractiveness'. In Murray, J. & Abramson, P.R. (Eds.) *Bias in Psychotherapy*. Praeger, New York, 1983.

34. Bar-Tal, D. & Saxe, L. 'Physical Attractiveness and Its Relationship to Sex-Role Stereotyping' *Sex-Roles*. 2, 1976, 123-133.

35. Searles, H.F. 'Oedipal Love in the Counter-Transference' *International Journal of Psychoanalysis*. 40, 1959, 180-190.

36. Scheflen, A.E. 'The Significance of Posture in Communication Systems' *Psychiatry*. 27, 1965, 316-331.

37. Howard, K.I., Orlinsky, D.E. & Hill, J.A. 'The Therapist's Feelings in the Therapeutic Process' *Journal of Clinical Psychology*. 25, 1969, 83-93.

38. Davidson, C.V. 'Making the Conceptual Leap from Sex Bias to Counter-Transference: A Closer Look at the Patient-Therapist Dyad'. In Murray, J. & Abramson, P.R. (Eds.) *Bias in Psychotherapy*. Praeger, New York, 1983.

39. Kernberg, O.F. *Borderline Conditions and Pathological Narcissism*. Aronson, New York, 1975.

40. Lakovics, M. 'Classification of Counter-Transference for Utilisation in Supervision' *American Journal of Psychotherapy*. 37, 1983, 245-257.

41. Argyll, M. *The Psychology of Interpersonal Behaviour*. Penguin Books, London, 1967.

42. Hall, E.T. *The Hidden Dimension*. Doubleday, Garden City, 1966.

43. Rosenthal, R., Hall, J.A., Archer, D., Di Matteo, R. & Rogers, P.L. 'The PONS TEST: Measuring Sensitivity to Non-Verbal Cues'. In Weitz, S. (Ed.) *Non-Verbal Communication*. Oxford University Press, Oxford, 1979.

44. Exline, R.V. 'Explorations in the Process of Person Perception: Visual Interaction in Relation to Competition, Sex and Need for Application' *Journal of Personality*. 31, 1972, 1-20.

45. Goz, R. 'Women Patients and Women Therapists: Some Issues That Come up in Psychotherapy'. *International Journal of Psychoanalytic Psychotherapy*. 2, 1983, 298-319.

46. Hoffman, M.L. 'Sex Differences in Empathy and Related Behaviour' *Psychological Bulletin*. 84, 1977, 712-722.

47. Weissman, M. & Klerman, G.L. 'Sex Differences and the Epidemiology of Depression' *Archives of General Psychiatry*. 34, 1977, 98-111.

48. Scarf, M. *Unfinished Business*. Fontana, Glasgow, 1981.

49. Kaplan, A.G., Brooks, B., McComb, A.L., Shapiro, E.R. & Sodano, A. 'Women and Anger in Psychotherapy' *Women and Therapy*. 2, 1983, 29-40.

50. Bardwick, J.M. & Douvan, E. 'Ambivalence: The Socialisation of Women'. In Gornick, V. & Moran, B.K. (Eds.) *Women in Sexist Society*. Basic Books, New York, 1971.

51. Unger, R.K. *Female and Male*. Harper & Row, New York, 1979.

52. Kaplan, A.G. 'Towards an analysis of sex-role related issues in the therapeutic relationship' *Psychiatry*. 42, 1979, 112-120.

53. Greene, L.R. 'On Terminating Psychotherapy: More Evidence of Sex-Role Related Countertransference' *Psychology of Women Quarterly*. 1980, 548-557.

54. Leonard, M.M. & Collins, A.M. 'Woman as Footnote' *Counselling Psychologist*. 8, 1979, 6-7.

55. Brodsky, A.M. 'The Consciousness-raising Group as a Model for Therapy for Women.' In Howell, E. & Bayes, E. (Eds.) *Women and Mental Health*. Basic Books, New York, 1981.

56. Carter, C.A. 'Advantages of Being a Woman Therapist' *Psychotherapy, Theory, Research and Practice*. 8, 1971, 297-300.

57. Mogul, K.M. 'Overview: the Sex of the Therapist' *American Journal of Psychiatry*. 139, 1982, 1-11.

58. Gilbert, L.A. 'Towards Mental Health: The Benefits of Psychological Androgyny' *Professional Psychologist*. 12, 1981, 29-38.

Residential Care of Adolescents: Residents, Carers and Sexual Issues

Keith White

INTRODUCTION

Most children in residential care in Britain are adolescents: 78 per cent of children in community homes are 13 years old or over [1]. One of the most important drives in adolescence is the sexual instinct. Most reports and research in the area, however, tend to regard sex as marginal or tangential. This is the most obvious and chronic problem that confronts any review of the relevant literature on practice, and it seems important to explore this inconsistency and to discover what it may mean before examining the little that has been written on the subject. Following this, I shall look at the two models which provide the basis for residential care of adolescents, both of which are problematic for sexual relationships and sexual expression. I will analyse the problems within three categories, and then proceed to specific practical issues like sex education, the Gillick case and Kincora.

THE IMPORTANCE OF SEX IN THE LIVES OF ADOLESCENTS AND THE ABSENCE OF REFERENCES IN RESEARCH AND REPORTS

In *Human Aggression*, Anthony Storr writes:

> 'For the majority of the human race, self-esteem is chiefly rooted in sexuality . . . . the object of physical passion is thus not only a means whereby the desire of sexuality can be expressed and assuaged, but it is a vital source of self-esteem' [2].

Whatever view is held of latent sexual feelings and expression in infancy, there is no doubting the fact that the sexual drive, coupled with the practical quest for self-esteem and identity, is particularly potent in adolescence.

The cultural climate in which British adolescents live is permeated by images and discussion of 'sex' whether in films, advertisements, newspapers or magazines. It is simply not an issue which it is possible to evade or ignore. (It is outside the scope of this chapter to examine the nature and quality of this saturation of our society, but it is important for the writer to register his personal concern about the marketing of sex as a commodity, its degrading approach to women, and the wrenching of sex from emotional, moral and religious contexts.)

How far this media climate reflects, and how far it has created, present-day sexual behaviour is one of the many imponderable questions posed in debate about sexual norms and values. Not surprisingly, however, whichever view is taken, any studies of adolescent sexual behaviour confirm the considerable sexual knowledge and experience admitted.

The WHO report, *The Problems of Children of School Age (14-18 Years)* [3], concluded that in the UK a quarter of 15 year olds regularly engage in genital apposition, and that ten per cent have engaged in sexual intercourse.

C. Farrell [4] reckoned that one in eight girls have sexual intercourse before the age of 16 years (i.e. 40,000 a year). Now although figures are not available, it would seem perfectly logical to conclude that the figures and percentages relating to children in residential care are higher, perhaps considerably higher, than these general data might suggest. And, of course, for all those adolescents not represented by such statistics, the understanding and experience of sex is still a major issue.

It comes as no surprise therefore to learn that in daily living in group care, the management of sexual drives, approaches, fantasies, is perhaps the most pressing practical task for staff and clients. It has affected the design of accommodation and sleeping arrangements. In their article 'Gender and the Pursuit of Respectability: Dilemmas of Daily Life in a Home for Adolescents', Howard Harris and Alan Lipman [5] found in a small group home they studied that bedrooms for boys and girls were in zones at opposite ends of the building separated by staff bed-sitting rooms. This spatial segregation was reinforced by an electronically operated lock and warning device. Interestingly enough, this home was originally designed as a mixed group home, but as a senior house-parent commented:

> 'If the architect had worked in residential care with teenagers, he wouldn't have planned for mixed groups. If the ends were mixed, they would be popping in and out of bed with each other' [5]. p.269.

Len Davis [6] gives several examples of sexual activity between staff and residents that occurred, but never came to light, within establishments or organisations.

What is not perhaps realised by those who have not experienced the group care situation first-hand is how much of daily living and planning revolves around the issue of sexual behaviour, taboos and fears. Any member of staff at any time is worried about being alone with any child. This is not just in N. Ireland, post Kincora, but has long been the case in the care of adolescents. Harris and Lipman [5] discovered this quite clearly (p.268):

> 'I won't go along the girls' corridor, or into the girls' common room or bedrooms without an Aunt with me, otherwise I might land myself on a charge of sexual assault' – Junior House Parent.

If someone is woken up by noise from girls in the middle of the night 'he must have a woman member of staff with him to protect himself from allegations of rape' – Deputy Officer-in-Charge. It affects every moment of day and night in establishments and, of course, any trips or expeditions outside them. It is one of the conscious and incongruous frameworks of any contact between staff and residents. This following extract from an internal memorandum is an eloquent reminder of the all-pervasive nature of the problem, listing hazardous situations:

> 'Car journeys, especially fairly long ones, taken by a man with a disturbed, sexually aware girl, or a young woman driving alone with a teenage boy . . . Staff should not make a habit of wandering about the house, or go into children's bedrooms to say Good-night, or get them up in the morning when dressed in pyjamas and dressing gown . . . Staff should be careful to safeguard their interests in situations in which they are in close proximity. For example, it is unwise for a male member of staff to have a 10 or 11 year old boy on his knee, with the lad dressed only in pyjamas' [5]. p.269.

There is no reason to suppose that what Harris and Lipman found is atypical of residential care for adolescents in general. Hence one would expect a good deal of information, research and reports on the subject. Instead it is one of the most neglected areas of residential care. It occurs, of course, after scandals like Kincora [7] but not in more routine assessments or descriptions. For example, the DHSS Inspection of Community Homes [1] barely mentions it. The main concern is with contraception and contraceptive advice [1, p.53]. The concomitants of sexual expression, aggression and violence, have received much more attention (e.g. Tutt [8]), but sex is the poor relation. It is a classic case of the literature and the policy-makers being completely out of touch with the realities at grass-roots level.

It is important before examining what has been written and analysed to speculate about the reasons for such a huge gap or incompatibility. Possible explanations include:

(1) The private nature of sexual experience. It is, of course, difficult for outsiders to discover what is really happening in this aspect of life. However open the issue may be to residents and between them, it will not be shared openly with others.

(2) The tendency of inspections and reports to focus on tangible issues like treatment plans, frequency of supervision, case reviews, records, length of stay. It requires lengthy residence in establishments to discover the sensitive issues in daily living. It is a reminder of how irrelevant what seem to researchers to be vital issues are to insiders and vice-versa.

(3) The issue is such a hornet's nest that it seems to be left alone consciously rather than by default. It involves personal norms and values and is not easily set in a context by which it can be assessed and which others agree is morally acceptable.

(4) According to Davis' findings there is so much clandestine sexual behaviour hidden for fear of punishment that it is a closed book as far as many staff are concerned. Perhaps existing behaviour and norms are totally out of keeping with public and organisational expectations.

Whatever the reasons, we cannot but remark on the readiness of the media to pick on any scandal of a sexual nature affecting adolescents in care, while the professionals in social work seem to give it such scant attention. It is all the more remarkable when one considers the comparatively thorough coverage of this issue as far as care of the handicapped is concerned. Perhaps more thought is needed on why 'sex and the handicapped' is a safer subject than 'sex and the adolescent'. It may be because it can be distanced from ourselves in relation to the handicapped. We can talk of 'them' rather than 'us'.

THE PREDOMINANT MODELS FOR RESIDENTIAL CARE OF ADOLESCENTS

There have been many experiments and many different types of residential group care for adolescents ranging from therapeutic communities to centres of behaviour modification, but the vast bulk of care provided is underpinned by one (or both) of two models: the family and the residential school. I say both because it is possible for a place to operate according to both models at any given time and it is also likely that, *over* time, the influence of one model may be superseded by the other.

The family model, so dominant after the Curtis Committee Report [9] in 1946, was the inspiration of a whole generation of 'family (small) group homes'. It took the ordinary nuclear family as its ideal and sought to adopt its patterns and lifestyle as much as possible. So 'quasi-families' were established, headed by married couples, with children of both sexes and a mixture of ages. Where possible they lived in ordinary houses that could not be distinguished from those of their neighbours. Foster care is the logical extension of the model and was seen by the Barclay Report as a type of residential care [10].

The school model which has underpinned approved schools and List 'D' schools as well as community homes, accepts that the creation of quasi-families is problematic. So special buildings, with particular treatment programmes organised by specialist trained staff, were established. The establishments might be single sex (like public boarding schools) or, on occasions, mixed; in size about 40 plus; with education sometimes on the premises. The environment was to provide a planned framework of care and treatment, in the same conscious way that a curriculum or syllabus is planned.

These are models or ideal types and it is not intended that they should describe actual establishments. They represent the ideals, the principles behind establishments past and presnt. They have had their own special problems in respect of sexual matters and it is to these in turn that we must move.

(a) *Sexual Relationships in the Family Model Establishments*

Between residents. The obvious basic problem is that residents are supposed to behave like brothers and sisters when they are not. This becomes more of a problem when one realises that most 'small group homes' now are effectively adolescent units. Younger children might be able to accept the sibling mythology but sexually mature teenagers cannot. Most such homes would actively discourage sexual relationships between children even if they were legally acceptable, the reason being that none of the normal controls of separate families and separate residences are operating. On the other hand, there are those who argue that it may be possible to exert more control in children's homes than on the streets and that 'natural' sexual expression should not be stamped out. It is enough to point out, however, what the reaction of natural parents, or the public, would be if a child were conceived by consenting adolescents in a small group home.

Between staff. This is a subject where nothing seems to have been written and yet similar problems obtain. The nuclear family is based on the fully intimate relationship between mother and father. They normally share a bed and spend much time together day and night. While small group homes were run singly by a married couple (with a little support and back-up) there was little problem relating to their sexual contact, except perhaps the lack of privacy (and energy) due to the nature of their life in that setting. As the staff teams grew, so did the potential for problems concerning sexual relationships. Many staff have formed close relationships on the job. As most staff live off the premises and 'sleeping in' rotas normally allow for just one person on duty, the extent of the contact between adults is nothing like as close or continuous as that between the children. But the problem of the irrelevance of the family model of care to the relationship of adults on the staff team remains.

Between staff and children. We have highlighted the problems already. The family group home is seeking to model itself on the nuclear family, but in the latter there are sexual taboos on the relationships between parents and their natural children. The absence of such taboos in family group homes and the corresponding absence of clear policy statements by employing organisations and professional associations leaves the door wide open to every form of problem. Len Davis has also put his finger on the problem that staff dare not raise the issue with anyone in their line management for fear of reprisal. In the absence of figures or documentation we must speculate, but the one example of an admitted sexual liaison between a staff member and resident would seem unlikely to be unique. The attitudes towards such situations range from a complete rejection of the principle that a full sexual relationship can be beneficial, to those who would welcome it as positive and therapeutic.

Between residents and others. This is an area where the family group home most nearly approximates to the ordinary nuclear family. Different families will have different values, but in nearly all cases contact between children of opposite sexes will not be discouraged. The issue then becomes how intimate, how frequent and how permanent that contact should be. The problem most often identified in relation to children in care is that many have been so deprived of consistent and loving care that they tend to be naturally promiscuous, seeking for a security in relationships often through sexual liaisons with a series of partners. In her book *Sexuality and Birth Control in Social and Community Work*, Elphis Christopher [11] makes this point both by a general statement and an illustrative case history. She rates girls in care as 'one of the most vulnerable groups of young people. . . . at particular risk of becoming pregnant in their early teens. Fourteen per cent of unmarried mothers in Harringey between 1968-76 had been in care for a substantial part of their childhood'.

In addition to the desire for affection, there is the attraction of a child of your own. A child who had been in care throughout childhood, now an unmarried mother, speaking of her son, told me: 'At last and for the first time I feel I have something that is my very own.'

Different attitudes to discos and youth clubs are, of course, in evidence, as with parties and nights out. There is little here, however, unique to family group homes.

(b) *Sexual Relationships in the Residential Schools*

Here the type of establishment is much more varied than the family group homes. Basically we are talking about places with education on the premises, often with residents of the same sex. The establishments are often a supplement to care in their own homes, with holidays, if not weekends, spent at home. If not, the likelihood that the period a child is at an establishment may be specific and limited.

Between residents. There is little here that has not been long-known and observed in relation to public and boarding schools. The children are not expected to behave as brothers or as sisters, because they are not, and the school model nowhere presupposes that this is how they should feel. However, many such establishments are isolated and the need for human warmth and contact manifests itself in homosexual relationships, usually not of a serious or lasting nature. The problem in addition to this is that sex is one of those issues and subjects shared exclusively among the resident peer-group: it is rarely on the formal agenda of the whole establishment. Sexual attitudes and behaviour are therefore not shaped by the caring adults but by the other young people. Exposed to merciless sexual exploitation by the media, it is doubtful whether this peer group influence can be positive.

Between staff. Apart from the isolation of such establishments, there are few situations that are any different from those faced by adults in other types of work and employment. It is possible to have a private family life without fear of intrusion, for the model is not dependent on the shared emotional life of staff and children, except in certain establishments seeking to live as therapeutic communities.

Between staff and residents. It is here that some of the most publicised situations have arisen. Lonely staff, some perhaps with intent, can form sexual relationships with young people and keep them hidden from colleagues, and by blackmail, suppressed by the young people themselves. The focus of attention has been largely on ways of screening adults seeking to enter such settings and this has gathered momentum since the Kincora case (see below) but the fact is usually accepted that there is no foolproof way of preventing the problem. Mixed schools may avoid it more than single-sex establishments.

Between residents and others. Certain establishments of this type, as we have noted, are isolated and they face the real difficulty that there is little contact possible with adolescents outside the establishments. More usually there is such contact and it becomes very difficult to regulate. A shift system of staff is not the best and most sensitive mechanism for evaluating and supporting or curbing an intimate ongoing relatioship. One member of staff told me that any overt sign of sexual relationships in his establishment meant that the young people were turned out on to the streets. The theory seemed to be that anything that happened there couldn't be held to be the fault of the staff, whereas anything on the premises could be held against them. This negative approach is probably very common. In effect the youngsters (both within and outside the establishment) are largely left to their own devices.

Some establishments will offer contraceptive advice and encourage the use of contraceptives. Others, notably the Christian-based establishments, seek to encourage chastity outside of marriage. The issue is not one that has been greatly debated by the protagonists.

We have tried briefly to outline the particular issues and problems common to each of the different models of residential child care. It is important to stress that we have dealt with ideal types rather than actual establishments, in order to isolate the aspects of sexual behaviour most pertinent to each type. We have not covered fostering but assume that many of the problems of family group homes are true, a fortiori, in foster homes. The relationship between break-downs and sexual issues has not, as far as I know, been explored, but it is an area which might usefully be studied as one would surmise it to be more important than has hitherto been suspected or reported.

Although it is not the primary purpose of this chapter to explore the issue of gender and sexist roles and values, it is important in practice as well as policy. There is an overarching problem in that residential child care itself, compared with fieldwork, can be seen as a typically feminine occupation, associated as it is with domestic work and nurture (as distinct from employed labour). The status of residential child care in Britain has never been on a par with fieldwork despite many significant efforts to improve its lot, and this would tend to encourage the conclusion that this is in some measure due to its link, largely unconscious, with the female/subservient stereotype. Certainly it has usually been the fieldworker, calling in at the home for meetings, who has called the tune and been invested with the power of decision making about a child's future. This gender-bias may help to explain certain aspects of children's consciousness while in residential care: a feeling of powerlessness, of being tied to a building, of being a passive recipient of decision making rather than a participant.

When applied to the two models above, gender issues become more focussed. In the family model there is the important question of the sex of the staff, their respective roles and how they relate to each other as models for the children and young people. The nuclear family has been a battleground for those seeking the source of sexist attitudes, and small group homes are faced with a number of critical decisions about status and roles. There will be decisions about who does the cooking, the washing, the domestic work, the maintenance; how dependent or independent each person is in a marriage relationship; who makes the decisions and how; what sort of controls are exercised and by whom; whether to acquiesce in relation to the unequal status afforded to fieldworkers and so on.

The school model may well have particular problems with sexist stereo-typing. It is likely that the domestics are all women and the maintenance and teaching is largely carried out by men; that senior staff will be men. Types of regimes, from 'hierarchical' to therapeutic, may well owe much to the gender question. Decision about what language and behaviour is acceptable will relate to gender too.

The purpose of this short discussion of sexist attitudes and gender is to note how big an issue it is in the residential care of adolescents and how artificial it is to see 'sex' as in some way unrelated to gender.

The final section of this chapter is devoted to three specific issues that affect every sort of residential care for adolescents.

SEX EDUCATION

When former residents gave evidence to the Hughes Enquiry [7] it transpired that a number of them had received no formal sex education at all (p.337). This is hardly surprising given their chequered and unplanned moves from one establishment to another. It would seem probable that one of the breakdowns in communication between adolescents in care and their parents concerns sex education. Once more the sensitive nature of sexual feelings, the privacy surrounding sexual expression and behaviour tend to mean that it is the subject of intentional neglect. When children move into care, it often results in a break in their schooling and thus any programme of sexual education may be missed. Thus when they arrive in care it is possible that home and school have not yet provided them with basic and structured sex education.

In care they will receive the distilled wisdom of the peer-group and the assault of the media, but the natural sexual conversations of the ordinary family related to, say, the birth of a new child, courtship of an older sibling, and the opportunity to pop into mum and dad's bed in the morning, with all its relaxed intimacy, are now proscribed. In any sort of residential establishment natural sexual contact and conversation is likely to be the same. Hence the need for a structured education plan: 'systematic arrangements should be made to provide children in residential care with suitable, considered instruction on the basic facts of life; on the dangers of sexual exploitation by adults; and on the health risks associated with sexual activity' [7] p.337.

Good contact with local schools will certainly help to make sure that there are no glaring gaps, but as Len Davis [6] points out, the education programme is predicated on the assumption that children are living in families. It is one thing to talk openly with such young people about every aspect of sex; quite another when the young people will be living side by side with members of the opposite sex and, therefore, with unusually frequent opportunities to explore and experiment. This relationship between ordinary school sex education and the needs of adolescents in care has not been given the attention it deserves.

As far as sexual counselling or sex education within establishments are concerned, the difficulty is in trying to be systematic yet not institutional. The DHSS inspectorate found that some establishments had formed discussion groups, some had found personal ways of helping young people to understand their own sexual development, and at least one place where a community nurse visited with a complete sex education programme including films and discussion sessions. Significantly, however, this section of the report is under the heading of 'Health Care: special needs', rather than 'Life in the Home: Daily Life'. The social and psychological nature of sexuality is not yet grasped right through the system.

One is left with the impression that the whole issue is one which is treated on a hit or miss basis. It is doubtful whether in any local authority, or most voluntary organisations, there would be enough common ground of ethics and values to allow a particular view of sex to permeate the life of an establishment. The result is almost certainly that young people in care are doubly deprived (to use Peter Righton's phrase [12]), first because of separation from home, second, because the care process is handicapping in itself. There is possibly no clearer demonstration of this than in relation to sex education.

THE GILLICK CASE AND CONTRACEPTION

In 1984 Mrs Gillick won her case at the Appeal Court against the local Health Authority and the DHSS. In essence she won the assurance that none of her daughters under 16 would be given contraception without her consent. The Lords overturned this decision in 1985, but with certain caveats and reservations. The net result is that doctors are reluctant to prescribe contraception without parental consent. The whole debate has centred on children in ordinary families and the balance between parental authority, a young person's independence and maturity, and the confidential nature of the relationship between a GP and client. The problem for children in care is that the whole balance is already skewed. (The issue is discussed briefly but effectively in 'Consent to Advise' by Nicholas Murray [13], though written before the Lords decision.)

The questions unique to the residential setting for adolescents are: Is it desirable to seek the consent of all natural or step parents? Who in the Local Authority or Voluntary Organisation is best placed to provide such consent? What importance should be attached to the child's stated religion? Is chastity outside of marriage a realistic or desirable goal for children in care? Isn't the privacy between young person and doctor one of the most valuable indicators of the trust a personal relationship requires, to children whose trust has been betrayed and who live in a far from private setting? Does contraception encourage promiscuity in some young people, particularly bearing in mind how close they live to each other? How do you balance health risks against psychological problems?

The legal debate has very big implications for those in residential care, which is why parts of the DHSS inspectorate findings on the matter are so disappointing.

> 'There were many homes where this matter, in the context of developing sexuality, had not been considered and was dealt with on an ad hoc basis and without advice' [1] p.53.

At the outset of the chapter the disparity between the importance of this subject and the lack of attention paid to it by the formal carers was outlined. The state of sex education, including contraceptive advice for children in care, is a firm indicator of the problem.

KINCORA

On 31st December, 1985, the Hughes Enquiry [7] reported on what was known as the Kincora scandal which involved chronic homosexual offences by three members of care staff at the Kincora Boys' Hostel in East Belfast, but also offences in other residential establishments. Among other things the affair demonstrated how difficult it is to get facts on sexuality if you are outside a residential setting; how the media and public react when something goes wrong in care; how sexuality has dominated and will dominate (in a different sense) the daily experience of care for most adolescents in care.

The enquiry makes 56 recommendations, all of which taken together involve a much tighter system of management control and clearly spelt-out procedures. In the circumstances it is difficult to see what other steps could have been taken, but in Northern Ireland now and on the mainland, the moves to tighten up systems to prevent sexual abuse are not going to help the healthy sexual development of young people in care. Everyone is looking over his or her shoulder. Natural, spontaneous sexuality is ruled out. The double deprivation of those in care will increase, though excesses in relation to some individuals will hopefully be weeded out.

This is one enquiry involving a few members of staff and residents. The vast majority of establishments have, of course, avoided such sad and destructive events and incidents. Yet they have not been unaffected. The whole climate is now more than ever one of safety-first. Every situation must be thought through. Any touch or show of affection is liable to be avoided. One-to-one chats in bedrooms are a thing of the past (think of that!). Sexual fear has become one of the primary factors in shaping daily living.

CONCLUSION

Generally speaking, there are now guidelines affecting the type and degree of corporal punishment, discipline or restraint in the residential care of adolescents. There do not seem to be guidelines of a similar nature for sexual contact and relationships. This may well be because such relationships are more complex, less amenable to any detailed regulation. It may be for this very reason that the matter is continually swept under the carpet, or it may be more deeply embedded in gender and power issues. The way forward is not easy to chart, but one step that would improve the present situation would be for the issue to receive the attention at management level that it now has on the ground. Perhaps it is too hot for the managers to handle in terms of its untidiness and risks and that is why it never gets priority on management agendas.

There is no doubt that many young people and the adults caring for them have successfully negotiated the problems stated here. It is equally true that many have been thwarted in their growth and development because of the problems mentioned. They are not easy to address or solve, but we must ensure that they are on everyone's agenda, not just when a crisis or crime occurs, but in the course of daily living. This will open up huge debates about the place of sex and power in care, what is public and private, what is morally acceptable. The alternative is an increasingly sterile, superficial life in care, where sex is something dirty, below the surface – a far cry from the beauty and freedoms with which it is rightly associated.

References

1. Social Services Inspectorate (DHSS). *Inspection of Community Homes*. DHSS, 1985.

2. Storr, A. *Human Aggression*. Penguin, 1968. [Quoted in Davis, L. *Sex and the Social Worker*. Heinemann Educational Books, 1983, p.15].

3. World Health Organisation. WHO Report: *The Problems of Children of School Age (14-18 Years)*. WHO, Copenhagen, 1978. [Quoted in Davis, L., 1983, p.14].

4. Farrell, C. *My Mother Said*. Routledge and Kegan Paul, London, 1978. [Quoted in Davis, L., 1983, p.14].

5. Harris, H. & Lipman, A. 'Gender and the Pursuit of Respectability: Dilemmas of Daily Life in a Home for Adolescents' *BJSW*. 14, 1984, 265-275.

6. Davis, L. 'Sex and the Residential Setting'. Ch.23 in Walton & Elliott, *Residential Care: A Reader*. Pergamon, 1980.

7. *Report of the Committee of Inquiry into Children's Homes and Hostels* (The Hughes Report). HMSO, Belfast, 1986.

8. Tutt, N. *Violence*. DHSS, Social Work Service Development Group (sponsor) and Norman Tutt (Editor). HMSO, London, 1976.

9. *Report of the Care of Children Committee* (The Curtis Report). HMSO, Cmnd. 6922, 1946.

10. *Social Workers – Their Role and Task* (The Barclay Report). Published for the NISW by Bedford Square Press, 1982.

11. Christopher, E. *Sexuality and Birth Control in Social and Community Work*. Temple Smith, 1980.

12. Righton, P. 'Sex and the Residential Social Worker' *Social Work Today*. 8, 19, 15th February 1977.

13. Murray, N. 'Consent to Advise' *Community Care*. March 7, 1985, 20-21.

Responding to the Sexuality of People with a Mental Handicap

Linda Coley and Richard Marler

REPRESSING OR FACILITATING?

Historically, the sexuality of people with a mental handicap has largely been ignored. Where it has been considered, the response from 'carers' has been restrictive and protective.

In recent years there has been a growing understanding of the reality that people with a mental handicap go through the physical changes of puberty, the emotional experiences of adolescence, and grow to adulthood where they make the same kinds of relationships and have the same feelings, desires and expectations as the rest of the population. However, 'carers' may not respond in a facilitating or educative way and people with a mental handicap, left in ignorance, may cope with their sexuality in socially unacceptable ways. Lack of the skills needed in this area of life may lead to the following situations: inappropriate and indiscriminate affectionate behaviour; vulnerability to sexual exploitation; sexual behaviour in public. Instances where people with a mental handicap fall foul of the law are well documented and Ann and Michael Craft have led the way in this country in trying to understand the context in which this happens [1].

It is important to note that despite being deprived of understanding, teaching and help in many instances, the vast majority of people with a mental handicap cope well with their sexuality and make the most of limited opportunities.

The sexuality of people with a mental handicap is surrounded by myths. The 'Eugenic View' is based on a collection of assumptions:

> that the mentally handicapped have a greater fertility rate
> that their offspring will be mentally handicapped also

that they have a greater sex drive
that they are a danger to the rest of society.

This view is fuelled by the tenet that, if unchecked, the sexuality of mentally handicapped people will lead to 'national degeneracy' and an 'unfit society'. In the past, the 'Eugenic View' contributed to the policy of segregating mentally handicapped people – at first in asylums in the 1900s, later in large subnormality hospitals in isolated locations. It also led to restrictive practices such as sterilisation without consent and prohibition of marriage [2,5].

Although the Eugenic View is rarely expressed openly these days, such beliefs may nevertheless underly certain attitudes and assumptions held by 'carers' today.

The opposing viewpoint is one that stresses the rights and dignity of the individual [3]. It follows from important moves to return people with a mental handicap to the community, and maintain them in it, and the adoption of 'normalisation' principles first advocated by Wolfensberger [4]. These principles rest on recognition of the rights of people with a mental handicap to lead as normal a life as possible within a community. This is achieved by reversing the 'devaluing process' imposed by society and promoting and supporting valued personal behaviour, experiences and opportunities. Many authorities have suggested that if normalisation principles are going to be fully implemented, this has important consequences for the rights of people with a mental handicap with regard to sexuality and that professionals involved in providing services are going to have to respond. Wendy Greengross and others have challenged service providers to look at the needs of handicapped people in terms of 'rights' and 'entitlements' [6].

If a sexual life is the incontestable right of every person with a mental handicap, then they have rights too in terms of facilitation. The United Nations Declaration of the Rights of Retarded Citizens (despite being orientated towards American culture) is useful in pointing out the rights of an individual

> 'to such education, training, habitation and guidance as will enable him/her to develop his/her ability and potential to the fullest extent no matter how severe the degree of handicap.'

The right to sexual expression may be of little use to an individual if he/she has not been helped to understand it, nor given the right environment and opportunity to pursue it.

Ann Craft has sub-divided these rights into four main areas [7].

(1) The right to know – assistance to cope with one's sexual development; access to information about themselves, other people, emotions and appropriate social behaviour.

(2) The right to a humane, dignified environment and privacy.

(3) The right to be protected – in a sensitive way, in which consideration of the rights of the person with a mental handicap may need to be viewed as distinct from that of parents.

(4) The right to make relationships – to love, share and care; to experiment and take 'relationship risks' – sorrow, sadness and hurt.

The ability of service providers to look at individual clients' rights to a sexual life and their role as 'facilitators', has clearly been aided by the 'Sexual Revolution' in society and by a movement which has seen a shift in power from professionals to clients, as illustrated by the growth of parent pressure and the self-advocacy movement.

The 'Sexual Revolution' in some of its aspects has not necessarily helped people with a mental handicap (nor anyone else in fact). Pauline Fairbrother, a parent, has pointed out that the images presented by the media emphasise 'the body beautiful' and the apparent need to be attractive in order to be sexual. Some people with a mental handicap may not be able to 'see through' the media 'hype' and may be personally affected [8].

Various studies have shown how people with a mental handicap may be particularly susceptible to strongly communicated 'norms'. In a study of sex roles and people with a mental handicap the difference between real life and aspirations was particularly large [9]. Another study, of ESN(M) secondary age children, found attitudes were far more conservative than their peer group's norms with many expressions of attitudes such as 'homosexuals should be punished' [10]. It is reasonable to surmise that the children may be reflecting the cautious and over-protective influences of their educators and parents. They may also be motivated, like any devalued group in society, to adopt what they imagine are the acceptable and valued norms of society.

Various researches have found that many people with a mental handicap, whilst eager for sexual contact, are fearful, anxious and ignorant about sexual matters and – to an unusual extent – see sex belonging exclusively to marriage, a state which many feel incapable of attaining [11]. In this way many people deny themselves sexual expression. Faced with the negative attitudes of families, professionals and the general public – and the conservative norms set for them, there is often a denial of interest in sexuality.

Livock [12] rightly points out that the issue now is whether we are going to turn our attention to the level of understanding about sex amongst this group, or else change the rules for normative inclusion in our society. If people are going to be firmly embraced as full members of the community, not only must they be given information about sexuality but society itself must provide facilities which allow the realistic expression of it.

Much depends on the attitudes of parents and staff. Sex education is given by parents without their always knowing it, through the cues and messages provided by their models of behaviour. The individual starts his or her own sexual education as the body changes in puberty but, due to the restrictions of immobility and supervision, the handicapped child does not have the 'normal' resources such as library, cinema and, above all, friends with which to observe other behaviours and to experiment. The handicapped child looks towards his/her immediate surroundings which are usually hemmed in by adult figures. Although there is an increasing awareness amongst parents that their children may have sexual needs and problems, they are not always in the best position to respond.

On reaching adulthood, particular attitudes taken by non-handicapped figures can be very damaging:

(1) Treating adults with a mental handicap as perpetual children, referring to them as 'girls' and 'boys' and insidiously denying their adult sexuality.

(2) Laughing at individual displays of affection or emotion, denying their ability to make serious relationships.

(3) Ignoring or denying sexual awareness because it may be more comfortable or problem free for the 'carers'.

All the above attitudes contribute to a severe restriction of the individual's personal growth and dignity. While learning difficulties may impose limits on the social and emotional development of people with a mental handicap, these limits should not be set up by others on their behalf. The fact that learning disability may make it more difficult for an individual to develop and mature should not mean they have less help to do so. They should be given many and varied opportunities to learn, and allowed to take reasonable 'risks'. Unfortunately, the attitudes of parents and/or staff often prevent these opportunities being given.

Stewart's study quoted a parent as saying 'I treat him as a baby. If I caught him masturbating I should simply smack him' [13]. Although this is an extreme viewpoint, many parents become very anxious whenever there is a sign of sexual interest. Much anxiety is based upon anticipation of problems rather than actual misdeeds. Craft suggests that coming to terms with their sons' or daughters' sexuality may precipitate a crisis equal to the one when they were first told that their child was mentally handicapped [7]. Sexuality issues may revive old fears for parents of not being able to cope. There is often little help for parents to deal with these fears and there is clearly scope for parents to support each other and for sensitive individual counselling from professionals.

The attitudes of professionals, however, often contribute to restricted opportunities. Greengross suggests that the problems that sexuality poses for residential staff are:–

(1) Many homes are established and run on Christian principles, with high moral and religious values.

(2) Parents are also seen as expecting the highest standards of moral behaviour.

(3) Staff are under pressure to avoid any hint of scandal which might damage the unit's public reputation.

Residential staff simply find it easier to deny, seeing sexuality as a 'Pandora's Box' better left unopened [6].

Studies have found that, in hospitals, attitudes towards the sexuality of residents are less tolerant amongst sisters and charge nurses than nursing assistants and student nurses [3]. It is suggested that this is linked to professional hierarchy and degree of responsibility for 'carrying the can' for any undesirable consequences. In some subnormality hospitals, patients who engage in sexual activity are often referred to a consultant psychiatrist as 'problems', although the referral is usually made to ensure hierarchical 'cover' for more junior members of staff. There is evidence to suggest that similar forces pertain in social services hostels and homes.

The attitudes of people with a mental handicap themselves – many of whom have internalised the conservative views presented by key figures – collude with the cautious approach of professionals to impose severe restrictions on personal growth and freedom.

THE ISSUES FOR DAY AND RESIDENTIAL STAFF

Day Services

The role of day services for people with a mental handicap has changed significantly over the last ten years. A typical local authority-run Adult Training Centre would be housed in a single storey factory workshop and its sole aim and activity would be to improve work skills and provide sub-contract work for its 'trainees'. Two developments – changes in the open job market and extension of the range of handicap catered for in ATCs – have prompted a review of day care. This has led to a consideration of people's needs other than the acquisition of narrow 'work skills' and inevitably this has focused on social and educational needs. As part of the programme of training in personal independence, social skills and community knowledge, attention has been turned to people's need for sexual education.

In Day Centres, it is now generally accepted that some form of sex education is a legitimate part of the programme to be offered to people with a mental handicap. Many will have missed out on even basic education, as special schools have only recently included it in their own curricula; and many people – as is often the case in other areas of life – are not ready to absorb information until much later than their childhood years. In the area of sexuality there are almost endless topics to learn and discuss and therefore it is very 'normal' and 'adult' to concentrate on it as part of a life skills package.

Day centre staff are probably more suitably placed than residential staff to offer a structured group in which to give education and encourage discussion about sexuality. In group living situations, where it is difficult enough to give a personalised service, residential staff often prefer to work with individuals, giving a mixture of information and counselling. Although day staff are used to giving education in groups they sometimes ignore the possible need for people to talk individually and confidentially on a topic that is of intense personal interest. Individual counselling needs to be offered as part of a formal group teaching programme.

Structured groups giving sex education need to be led by two workers. However well trained, staff members inevitably impart their own values and beliefs into the content of the instruction. Two workers with different life experiences and from different backgrounds are more likely to give a group a more rounded view of sexuality in general; and to convey the idea that this is an area where much is owed to personal choice and experience.

Moreover, it is important for one worker at any single time to be free from giving information so that s/he can observe the effect on group members, and discern what is being understood, misinterpreted, giving relief or causing anxiety. This is particularly so in a group which includes people with communication difficulties, where facial expressions and body language provide the only feedback as to understanding. In any group, at least one of the co-leaders needs to be fully trained although it is quite valid for the second person to gain experience in an ongoing group before seeking suitable training courses. Various agencies now offer specialist training for staff [14].

Staff have found advantages to both single sex and mixed sex groups. In single sex groups it is quicker to go through the embarrassment and jocularity barriers to be able to hold open and sensible discussions. In mixed sex groups, the tendency is to tread more circumspectly and the discussion on some topics is less frank. It has been concluded that a structured group programme such as this is best organised on mixed sex lines with a male and female co-leader, with the opportunity to split into single sex sessions to cover certain areas and then to come back together and share experiences.

A full course of group education and discussion includes consideration of the following: self awareness and awareness of others; human development; emotions and feelings; social behaviour and attitudes; sexual activity; relationships; family planning; parenthood; counselling and guidance. Materials that are available for use with adults who have learning disabilities are in short supply. Any temptation to use resource material that has been created with children in mind needs to be overcome, as it is important – in line with 'normalisation' principles – to present age appropriate material. There is, however, a growing number of suitable slide sets, books and questionnaires which can be used selectively as part of a group programme [15].

Although day centres have a clear role to provide sexual education and counselling as part of their general social education programme, there are other issues that confront day centre staff.

For example, in day centres what should be the policy about sexual activity on the premises? Following normalisation principles, would it be inappropriate to permit it because the ATC or SEC is the equivalent of a non-handicapped person's workplace? But what about lack of opportunity – many handicapped people live at home with ageing parents and their main social opportunities happen during the daytime? Or they may live in a hostel which either does not have the facilities for, or discourages overnight visitors? Who is responsible if sex takes place at a day centre – can parents accuse staff, or is it the sole responsibility of the handicapped people themselves? What if one of the partners is more severely handicapped than the other – who decides whether she or he is in a position to give consent? These issues point to two important needs:

(1) The need for training of day care staff on sexuality issues.

(2) The need for a Policy and Guidelines to support and advise day centre staff.

Residential Services

Residential services to people with a mental handicap have similarly seen radical changes in ethos and location in the last ten years.

Historically, mentally handicapped people were locked away in asylums and latterly in large subnormality hospitals usually located in extremely isolated places. Alternative residences were provided by charities with similarly authoritarian and protective regimes. As more establishments have been opened in the community – by health authorities, voluntary organisations and local authorities – and a wider range of residential options has been offered to people with a mental handicap, so the approach to people's care and well-being has become more enlightened and more individualised. Service managers have tended to see more clearly the need for education and counselling in sexuality, since the move to provide 'core and cluster' living.

An important issue for residential staff is the temptation to hold onto the old authoritarian principles of care because of the dependency that many residents have on staff. In residential life, where it is almost impossible, and often undesirable, to maintain a 'professional' barrier, staff have particular difficulties in responding objectively to the sexuality of residents. For some staff 'sexuality' is allied to 'independence' and they are often all too aware of people's dependency. For others, because of the closeness of their working relationships with residents, the issue of sexuality is seen as a threat to their own personal space. A staff member may at various times be the object of sexual advances from a resident or at other times may feel attracted to a client. It is to be expected that these situations happen and there is no need for a staff member to feel guilty or feel they are responding unprofessionally. However, they do need good supervision which can offer help and support to work through these feelings.

Typical residential environments are not conducive to 'normal' opportunities for pursuing relationships. Even if they are mixed sex residences and have single rooms, there are rarely facilities for locking a bedroom door, sleeping in double beds, or having visitors stay overnight. Many establishments seem intent on creating a sentimental child-like environment with age-inappropriate posters and cuddly toys, etc. The lack of personalised space, individual decor and personal furniture and belongings reinforces people's dependency and lack of initiative. In establishments which are designed for observation and group living, it is not surprising that 'private' behaviours are played out in public.

In the same way that environment plays its part in facilitating or repressing sexuality, so does the establishment's regime. Because it is organisationally easier and economic in staff time to respond to people as a group, people are not encouraged to take up individual interests or go out in ones and twos to ordinary places. Therefore people tend to stay with the same group at the hostel or go as a group to the local Gateway Club where they will probably meet the same people they have spent the day with.

Many residential staff members are now tackling their role in a new way. They act from the basis of giving encouragement to individual decision-making by presenting choices, giving information to back it up and supporting when carried through. The result is probably a less efficient and less smooth running home. Nevertheless there is much evidence now that in places where emotional freedom and sexual expression are encouraged, the tensions of group living – indicated by arguments, aggression and temper tantrums – are considerably eased.

Residential staff have tended to offer individual teaching and counselling on sexual matters rather than organising structured groups. Although formal group work may help in giving basic education to all residents, it seems appropriate for residential staff to offer a personalised service for people who live in a group setting. The issues that confront residential staff are various and many. What should be the policy about intervention if one resident appears to be sexually exploited by another? If 'informed consent' is not available due to severity of handicap, who decides – parent or professional – about such things as contraception and sexual opportunity? In being given intimate personal care, what if a resident becomes sexually aroused? There are no easy answers to such questions for residential staff and they point to the same needs expressed by day centre staff – the need for training and policy guidelines.

Although day and residential staff have really been the first to respond to the challenge of teaching and counselling people with mental handicaps in the area of sexuality, other professionals need to be encouraged to gain these skills in order to take advantage of their special position. In particular, Community Mental Handicap Team personnel – whether social worker, community nurse or psychologist – are well placed to offer this; and in other situations it is important for field workers, adult education staff and medical and para-medical staff at least to understand the principles and issues concerned.

RESPONDING TO THE ISSUES

Training

Professionals working closely with mentally handicapped people – and their families, need to respond carefully to the many issues raised by sexuality. Above all, they need training and policy guidelines in order to do so. A few authorities have policy statements [16] and many others are preparing their own. The issues are complex and the range of problems endless, but a policy can give staff a written framework of support, a set of principles from which to develop their own response to individual circumstances. In addition to supporting and guiding staff, a policy also protects the rights and interests of clients with a mental handicap.

In the interests of both staff and clients, there needs to be a clear understanding of the law [17]. The Mental Health Act (1983) excludes severely mentally handicapped people from being able to give consent to sexual intercourse although the main purpose of the law is to protect women with severe mental handicap from exploitation. Where there is no evidence of exploitation it seems most unlikely that the law would be invoked and indeed there are 'get out' clauses which would allow for most relationships to be untouched by the law.

Consent

Any policy statement needs to address itself to the question of 'informed consent'. This extends to the full range of sexual behaviours. Staff may need to intercede, for instance, where they feel a mentally handicapped person who is unable to communicate verbally, is unable to resist unwanted sexual advances. They need to be acutely sensitive to non-verbal communication in order to gauge a person's true wishes.

In other instances, parents may 'forbid' relationships despite the fact that both parties are consenting. Parents may have very special reasons for holding strong views about sexuality issues and the professionals involved need to be sensitive to the fact that they may need help to overcome them. Parents need to be offered opportunities to work in partnership with professionals at resolving such issues. Where there is conflict between parent and professional over a client's best interests, there is no easy resolution and the sad reality is that whoever has 'care' of that person has most power.

That power has been grossly abused, in even recent times and many women have been sterilised or had abortions without their consent being sought. The demand for sterilisation is sometimes insistent and can seem to be a very effective solution to a person's 'sexual problems'. It is a drastic and usually permanent process with serious implications for civil and legal rights. The well-being of the client needs to come first and since sterilisation is such a final step, the suitability of contraception needs to be explored extensively first. If sterilisation is the only reasonable option available, intensive counselling is needed so that the individual understands what is being proposed and is able to consider his/her present and future emotional needs. In a situation where a person with a mental handicap is unable to give consent, the law gives no guidance and often much depends on the decision taken by the medical profession.

The situation is different where an individual with a mental handicap is able to express his or her own wishes and where these are denied, there may be a need for advocacy – by parent or staff member – to support the decision. Advocacy is also an issue for professionals outside day and residential establishments. Where a person is not able or is not allowed to speak for her/himself, social workers need to question the policy and practice of carers with regard to sexuality issues and, if necessary, advocate on behalf of an individual. Volunteer advocates may also have an important role to fulfil in this respect.

The issue of 'informed consent' raises again the importance of continuing sex education and counselling being offered to people with a mental handicap so that they are in a position to choose for themselves from a knowledgeable position. Where formal education and training in sexual matters is difficult because of communication difficulties, poor concentration or severity of handicap, teaching happens 'in situ'. Staff and parents need to be aware that the way they respond to sexual behaviours is in fact a way of 'teaching' people about sexuality. Public displays of, for instance, petting or masturbation may need to be discouraged but staff need to ensure that they are not conveying that the activity is wrong, simply that the place may be wrong. Positive alternatives must be offered in a way that individuals will understand. Staff will need to be careful, however, not to actively facilitate sexual expression to the extent of their own personal involvement. The teaching of masturbation, for example, might be seen as helpful but difficult to engineer in the classroom. Teaching 'in situ', however, is likely to lead to misunderstandings and may indeed be illegal.

Staff also need to be aware that people with a mental handicap are as likely as the non-handicapped population to indulge in the whole range of sexual activity. Homosexual behaviour in institutions has in the past been viewed as evidence of moral degeneracy (the Eugenic View) and there is evidence to suggest that staff may in fact expect more homosexual activity than heterosexual activity, although it may not make them more tolerant than the general public [18]. As with the general population, men and women with mental handicaps may show interest in either or all of heterosexual, homosexual and bisexual activity. Staff attitude is important, and they need to be aware that they can engender unnecessary guilt and feelings of 'deviancy' if they react in a way that is disapproving.

Staff also need to beware of 'categorising' someone on the basis of behaviour alone, unless an individual her/himself chooses a label. Homosexual behaviour may be an occasional or passing choice, as it is with many non-handicapped people, and again labelling people on this basis is inappropriate. Some people with a mental handicap may have turned to this choice because of forced segregation of the sexes in school or hospital ward; some people may feel less inhibited about society's sexual role 'straitjackets'.

Contraception

People with a mental handicap clearly have the right, so often denied them, to have full sexual relationships and the opportunity to pursue them in privacy. Contraceptive information needs to be available within an overall education programme – whether offered at a day or residential centre – but individual counselling may also be necessary either by direct care staff or family planning experts. Staff (and parents) need to ensure that people get the best possible medical advice and should facilitate visits to Family Planning Clinics. Every effort must be made to ensure that the client understands any contraceptive method advised. The situation where a client is given contraception without knowing or understanding what it is for, is to be avoided, except where someone's severe disabilities make communication on this point impossible. Where a client wants contraception, the client's wishes to inform parents or not should be honoured: where a client is unable to understand and take responsibility for contraception, a case conference including staff, parents, management officer and social worker needs to be called to decide what to do. The situation may be different for under 16 year olds. In all cases contraception needs to be viewed in terms of the needs and wishes of the client, rather than as a means of relieving the anxieties of staff or parents'. Male clients will be included, where appropriate, in education about the different contraceptive methods in order to promote male responsibility in the contraceptive process. They may need to be taught in what circumstances and how to use a sheath (using an artificial penis as model).

Marriage and Cohabitation

People with a mental handicap have the same rights as anyone else to marry or cohabit with someone. There is often very little willingness from staff or parents to facilitate this, partly because of attitude, partly because of the inflexible layout and furniture of most residences for people with a mental handicap. Most important, however, is attitude; if there were a greater willingness to accept that two people may wish to share a room and a bed, practical solutions would be found to accommodate the need. Some non-handicapped people seem to think that if cohabitation is sought then it is not a serious relationship; if marriage is sought, that the couple concerned do not have the intellectual understanding to make such a commitment. All the conscious or unconscious fears related to the 'Eugenic theory' may also come into operation. In many cases, for staff and parents it is simply easier to say 'no'.

There is no law specifically restricting the right of a person with a mental handicap to marry. Such a person who is over the age of 18 may marry so long as the Registrar of Marriages is satisfied that s/he understands the nature of what s/he is undertaking. The rights of 16-18 year olds are the same as those of non-handicapped teenagers.

Parenthood

Where couples or single women with a mental handicap wish to have children there is clearly a need for careful counselling. Although people with a mental handicap should not be expected to give guarantees on good parenthood in a way that is not expected of non-handicapped people, they may need to consider all the issues before taking a decision. They will need counselling on their expectations of parenthood, their experience of being parented, their ability to cope with child-rearing and the services available or unavailable to help in this. They will also have to consider the needs of the child and imagine what kind of life s/he would have. Genetic counselling from an expert may also be advisable. There is no clear evidence to suggest that people with a mental handicap are more likely to have handicapped children or that they will be inferior parents [1]. Although support systems may be essential, many people will have the help of family networks and community services.

Addressing the issue of 'parenthood' is relatively new for service providers and anxiety may therefore be understandably high. Wherever possible, the choice needs to remain with the people who in the end have to take that decision – those who are considering whether or not to become parents.

In the past, when a woman with a mental handicap has become pregnant the only option has been abortion. Unless health is severely at risk, every woman should be given the choice of abortion or childbirth. If abortion is chosen it needs to be carried out in a supportive atmosphere with sufficient information-sharing and counselling before and after, such as other women in society would hope. The law states that no abortion operation can take place on an adult (over 16) without her consent. There is, however, no definition of 'consent' or how much information needs to be given and understood before consent is sought. The law does not deal with incapability of giving consent. Where there is such a situation, the key figures in an individual's life need to be brought together in a case conference in order to take that decision.

CONCLUSION

People with a mental handicap have the right and need the freedom to enjoy their sexuality and have it recognised by others. As with non-handicapped people, they have a right to a sexual life, in line with the principles of normalisation and the United Nations Declaration of Rights. Moreover, they have a right to education and counselling relevant to their individual needs.

The issues raised for service managers, service providers and parents are enormous and complex. There are no easy answers but a response needs to be made. Training for staff, together with written policies and guidelines, can help professionals to make an appropriate response so that people with a mental handicap are allowed greater personal growth and freedom.

References

1. Craft, A. & Craft, M. *Sex and the Mentally Handicapped*. Routledge and Kegan Paul, London, 1978.

2. Craft, A. & Craft, M. *Handicapped Married Couples: a Welsh Study of Couples Handicapped from Birth by Mental, Physical or Personality Disorders*. Routledge and Kegan Paul, London, 1979.

3. Harvey, R. 'The Sexual Rights of Mentally Handicapped People' *Mental Handicap*. 11, 3, 1983, 123-125.

4. Wolfensberger, W. 'The Principle of Normalisation'. In *Human Services*. National Institute on Mental Retardation, Toronto, 1982.

5. Ufford Dickerson, M. 'Mental Handicap and Parenting: Rights and Responsibilities of Full Citizenship' *Canadian Journal on Mental Retardation*. 35, 2, Spring 1985.

6. Greengross, W. *Entitled to Love*. Malaby Press, London, in association with National Fund for Research into Crippling Diseases, 1976.

7. Craft, A. 'Sexuality and Mental Handicap' *Physiotherapy*. 71, 4, April 1985.

8. Fairbrother, P. 'Love and Affection' *Health and Social Service Journal*. 170, December 9th, 1977, 1684.

9. Lundstrum-Roche, F. 'Sex Roles and Mentally Handicapped People' *Mental Handicap*. 10, 1, March 1982, 29-30.

10. Watson, G. & Rogers, R. 'Sexual Instruction for the Mildly Retarded and Normal Adolescent: A Comparison of Educational Approaches, Parental Expectations and Pupil Knowledge' *Health Education Journal*. 39, 3, 7th November 1980, 88-95.

11. Heshusius, L. 'Sexuality, Intimacy and Persons we Label Mentally Retarded: What They Think – What We Think' *Mental Retardation*. 20, 4, August 1982, 164-168.

12. Livock, R. 'Developing a Sexual Policy' *Community Care*. June 7th, 1979.

13. Stewart, W.F.R. *Sex and the Physically Handicapped*. Action for Research for the Crippled Child, London, 1975.

14. Family Planning Association – first and second level courses, special packages; SPOD – Sexual and Personal Relationships of the Disabled; British Institute for Mental Handicap.

15. Winifred Kempton's slide sets: 'Sexuality and the Mentally Handicapped' 1978. Ann Craft's slide sets: 'Educating Mentally Handicapped People'; 'Health, Hygiene and Sex Education for Mentally Handicapped Children and Adolescents'. A review of audio-visual resources, 1980. Dr. J. Docherty: 'Growing Up: A Guide for Young people. 1982. Miller & Pelham? 'Facts of Life'. Kaye Wellings: 'First Love, First Sex'. J.J. Head: 'How Human Life Begins'. London Borough of Hounslow. 'Sexuality of Mentally Handicapped People – Guidelines for Staff', 1983.

16. London Borough of Camden. 'The Sexuality of People with a Mental Handicap' – Policy and Guidelines for staff working in London Borough of Camden establishments, March 1986.

17. Dixon, H. & Gunn, M. 'Sex and the Law – a brief guide to staff working in the mental handicap field'. England and Wales only, Nov. 1985. Family Planning Association Education Unit.

18. Adams, G., Tallon, R. & Alcorn, D. 'Attitudes Towards the Sexuality of Mentally Retarded and Non-Retarded Persons'. *Education and Training of the Mentally Retarded*. Dec. 1982.

Sexual Counselling

Bobbie Fraser

This paper looks at the nature and causes of adult sexual difficulties, known as sexual dysfunctions, and the aims and methods of treatment which are currently in use. Evolving approaches to the subject are well illustrated in the standard works of Masters and Johnson [1,2], Belliveau and Richter [3], Kaplan [4] and Bancroft [5].

Most people experience mild sexual dysfunction at some time during their lives, from fatigue, drugs, reduced drive, ill-feelings or other causes. Variations in sexual performance and pleasure are part of the normal scene. It is only where such variations become more obvious that the word sexual dysfunction should be used.

In the past, people were not inclined to seek help for their sexual difficulties and effective help was seldom available. The last 20 years, however, have brought remarkable advances in our knowledge of human sexual behaviour, and it is now widely recognised that many of these problems can respond to a relatively brief and focused intervention. There is now a great increase in the provision of treatment for sexual problems, and in the demand for it.

ADULT SEXUALITY

Our capacity to respond sexually is a natural function of our adult body: much of our current understanding of the human sexual response comes from the pioneering work of Masters and Johnson [1], who described a 'normal sexual response cycle' common to both men and women. A wide range of factors, however, can be expected to have an impact on our sexuality – our feelings about ourselves and our bodies, the attitudes and values we have acquired in our upbringing, cultural influences and the changing relationships with those closest to us. Coming to terms with our sexuality can be a process which unfolds smoothly and naturally. For many people, however, the area of sexuality remains unresolved or distorted throughout adulthood, leading to problems in personal relationships or avoidance of intimacy. Table 1 lists some common sexual misconceptions. Rushbridger [6] gives an amusing survey of changing fashions in popular sexual advice.

TABLE 1

Some Common Sexual Myths
(derived from Zilbergeld [7])

1. Men should not express their feelings.
2. It is performance that counts.
3. The man must take charge of and orchestrate sex.
4. All physical contact must lead to sex.
5. Sex equals intercourse.
6. Sex requires an erection.
7. A man always wants and is always ready to have sex.
8. Masturbation is dirty or harmful.
9. When a man gets an erection he must have an orgasm.
10. Sex should always be natural and spontaneous: talking about it spoils it.
11. Any man ought to know how to give pleasure to a woman.
12. Sex is really good only when partners have simultaneous orgasms.
13. If people love each other they will know how to enjoy sex together.
14. Partners in a sexual relationship instinctively know what the other partner thinks or wants.

Sex has many uses and abuses and is very much open to misinterpretation and conflicting messages. We can use our sexuality in positive ways – for pleasure, for intimacy, for communication, for childbirth or to bolster our sense of self-esteem, identity or attractiveness; and in negative ways – as an expression of anger, power or rebellion, commercial exploitation or as a means of flouting rules and conventions. Two people may engage in a sexual relationship for very different sets of reasons. Even within the same person, attitudes and values may vary widely throughout a lifetime, and the importance and significance of sexual pleasure varies considerably as our interests, relationships and life change. Sexual behaviour is therefore extremely variable within the same person and between people. there are, however, certain predictable sexual responses which have been identified and explored, particularly in the last 20 years, and it is the failure or fear of failure of these desired responses that gives rise to problems. Sexual problems, in this context, therefore refer to situations where the sexual performance of an individual or couple is impaired in such a way as to cause distress to either or both partners.

HOW DO SEXUAL PROBLEMS PRESENT?

Sexual problems present a range of difficulties from the simple, easy to help, to those that are more complex and intractable. They are many and varied and can occur at various points in the life-cycle and it is now recognised that there are certain times when people are specially at risk of developing sexual difficulties. They may be a source of considerable distress and can cause a number of other problems – depression, low self-esteem, relationship problems, marital and family breakdown. They may present in direct or indirect ways to helping agencies and can be expressed in a number of disguised forms. Frequently, marital problems present as sexual problems or vice versa. Some people disguise their problems as physical complaints: others experience sexual difficulties because of physical illness or disability. Because of the psychosomatic nature of sexual problems they can present in a wide variety of clinical settings. Bancroft and Coles [8] noted that the majority of people approach their GPs in the initial stages of seeking help. The decision to seek professional advice is a difficult one and the attitude of the professional to whom they first speak is probably crucial. Most people view sexual matters as private and intimate and are inhibited and embarrassed about discussing them with strangers. Many fear rebuff from their doctor and many are uncertain about whether they can be helped.

The prevalence of sexual problems is now known, reflecting, in part, the difficulties in obtaining reliable information about sexual behaviour. In addition, there are few objective criteria available to distinguish normal from abnormal. Several studies have attempted to explore the incidence of sexual problems, both in the general population and in the clinical population, the relationship between sexual problems and social class, and the complex connection between marital dissatisfaction and sexual dissatisfaction. Clinical experience suggests that the number of people seeking help for their sexual difficulties has increased greatly [9,10,11].

There are a number of factors which may be significant. Profound changes have taken place in society in the last 25 years. Sexual behaviour is now freely discussed by the mass media. The women's movement has emphasised the sexual rights and expectations of women and drawn attention to women's role in society. As a result, many women view their sexuality differently and have become more assertive.

This shift in attitudes and values has increased our self-awareness and expectations and resulted in much higher aims for personal fulfilment for both men and women. For many, however, the increase in their sexual expectations has led to dissatisfaction with themselves or their partners. It is likely therefore that this change in expectations explains, in part, the apparent increase in the prevalence of sexual problems.

HUMAN SEXUAL BEHAVIOUR

Research into sexuality has passed through a number of phases, the contributions of Freud, Marie Stopes, Havelock Ellis and Kinsey being the major influences throughout the first half of the 20th Century [12,13].

Havelock Ellis at the end of the 19th Century was the first to subject 'normal' sex to scientific investigation and documented all knowledge (or lack of it) about sex research at the time in his six-volume study of the psychology of sex. The early psychoanalysts were concerned to understand sexual phenomena against the background of Freud's *Essays on the Theory of Sexuality* [14], which contributes to the understanding of sexual dysfunction and sexual deviance. The contributions of ego psychologists have focused attention on personality factors and their relatiohsip with basic drives, conscience and the demands of the external world, e.g. Erikson [15] and Anna Freud [16].

Obtaining an accurate picture of human sexual behaviour is difficult because of the sensitive and highly personal nature of the information. Valid questions can be asked about the reliability of information, the precision of definition and to what extent the sample is representative. Despite these difficulties, there have been several large scale studies of contemporary sexual attitudes. Undoubtedly, the most influential of these were the Kinsey surveys in 1948 and 1953 [17,18] which proved a landmark and were the first serious attempt to obtain information on a large scale. Meaningful questions were asked of a defined sample of ordinary people to find out about sexual behaviour in general, and not just in those presenting with sexual problems to specialist clinics. Gebhard and Johnson [19] published a re-analysis of the Kinsey data with the addition of new data. Survey research was later aimed at special groups such as young people [20,21] and women [22,23].

From these and other studies began to emerge an acceptable classification of psychosexual problems in terms of sexual dysfunction and sexual deviance.

CLASSIFICATION OF SEXUAL PROBLEMS

It is widely recognised that the sexual response is a complex phenomenon in which psychological and physical processes interact and that sexual function is a prime example of a psychosomatic process [1,4,5]. Disturbances of either component may result in sexual problems, although there is a striking variation between individuals in their vulnerability to such problems. It is widely believed that psychological factors are the commonest and most important in disrupting sexual responses but there is no conclusive agreement about the nature of these factors and the specific connection between particular psychological factors and sexual dysfunction. Many people with sexual difficulties are free of other problems, while many people who have serious emotional conflicts, neurotic personalities or highly destructive marital relationships have functioning sexual relationships.

Evidence suggests that sexual dysfunction may be caused by a great variety of factors complexly related – that there is an interplay between the here-and-now factors which provoke anxiety, the personality of the individual which makes him vulnerable to the situation and makes it difficult for him to deal appropriately with these feelings, early family experiences, marital disharmony and culturally restrictive social attitudes. Cole [24] describes Bancroft's model of the psychosomatic circle as 'one of the neatest models to describe causation of sexual problems.' Fairburn et al. [25] illustrate this in this helpful diagram.

It is recognised that performance anxiety plans a very important role in sexual roblems. It is a response to sexual failure and it can perpetuate the problem long after the primary cause has ceased to exist. Performance anxiety encourages the individual to monitor his or her sexual performance which causes further deterioration in sexual functioning; a vicious circle is established and a dysfunctional pattern of behaviour is created and maintained. Any source of sexual failure may produce performance anxiety – the primary problem may be psychological or physical. Physical illness and disability may interfere directly with sexual activity; in other situations, the sexual difficulty is just one aspect of the psychological reaction to the physical problem.

As yet there is no satisfactory system for classifying sexual dysfunction which incorporates physical, psychological and interpersonal aspects. Masters and Johnson categorised problems in terms of genital and orgasmic responses and these categories have been widely adopted, although there is increasing awareness that they are not satisfactory. Kaplan [4,26] empha-

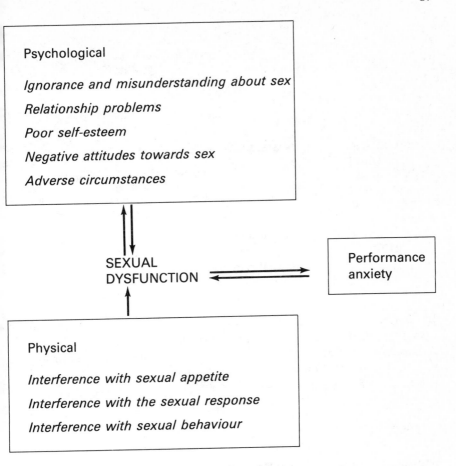

sised the need to distinguish between arousal and orgasmic phases and further distinguished sexual desire from arousal and orgasm. The following classification system is derived from Hawton [27] and Fairburn et al. [25].

Sexual problems may be categorised as primary or secondary. Primary problems are those present from the outset of sex, whereas secondary problems develop after a period of satisfactory sexual activity [2]. Often the partner's problems are inter-relational and it is not uncommon for both partners to be dysfunctional, e.g. it is quite common for premature ejaculation to be associated with general sexual unresponsiveness. Masters and Johnson also suggested the term 'situational' to describe a problem which occurs in one setting and not in another, and 'total' for problems which occur in all settings.

TABLE 2

Classification of sexual dysfunction
(from Hawton [27] and Fairburn? et al. [25]

Aspects of Sexuality Affected	Women	Men
Sexual interest	low sexual interest	low sexual interest
Arousal	poor sexual arousal	erectile dysfunction
Orgasm	orgasmic dysfunction	premature ejaculation retarded ejaculation
Other types of dysfunction	vaginismus dyspareunia sexual phobias low sexual pleasure	dyspareunia sexual phobias low sexual pleasure

In addition to specific dysfunction, it is also important to take account of sexual satisfaction which is another dimension of human sexuality. Frank and colleagues [28,29] highlighted the links between sexual satisfaction and aspects of the relationship both sexual and non-sexual other than the presence or absence of sexual dysfunction.

APPROACHES TO TREATMENT

During the second half of this century, there have been major changes in social and professional attitudes towards the treatment of sexual problems. 'The situation is still in flux but there is reason to think that progress towards a rational approach is being achieved' [5].

Up to 30 years ago, sexual problems, whether experienced as dysfunction or deviance, were seen as symptomatic of some more basic personality or neurotic problem or deep-rooted inner conflict and requiring some form of psychoanalytic treatment. The main alternative has its origins in the behavioural approach which became established in the 1950s to 1960s. The early emphasis was on aversive conditions and the modification of undesirable sexual behaviour – now there is much more emphasis on learning new patterns of behaviour rather than actively discouraging old ones. Exploration of the possibilities of surgical, pharmacological and mechanical methods of teatment has been a third strand of investigation. These contrasting approaches remained separate and little attempt was made to find a common perspective or to explore the possibilities of using different or combined approaches for different problems.

There was one interesting exception. In the 1950s Balint applied his psychoanalytic training to devise ways for GPs to achieve more limited aims in a short time with a wide range of problems [30]. Along with other family planning doctors, he developed sexual counselling techniques within the Family Planning Association and evolved a relatively brief approach to helping women with sexual difficulties, in particular non-consummation. This approach has thrived, though confined to doctors as therapists, and has become organised as the Institute of Psychosexual Medicine, offering training and treatment [31].

In 1970, Masters and Johnson published their book, *Human Sexual Inadequacy* [2], claiming impressive results in a large number of couples with sexual dysfunction, using intensive but brief treatment methods. They also produced follow-up data for at least five years. As a consequence of these studies there has been an explosion of interest in the treatment of sexual difficulties and the last two decades have brought remarkable advances in our knowledge which has made the pursuit of further knowledge about sexual functioning and methods of treatment respectable.

Some of their ideas were innovatory. They produced a systematic exploration of the human sexual response cycle. They focused on the couple; they used co-therapy; they formulated a rapid-treatment residential programme lasting two weeks using mutual pleasuring techniques (sensate focus exercises) and putting a ban on intercourse, followed by home assignments. They encouraged sexual communication between the couple and in so doing concentrated on the elimination of sexual myths, and they formulated a series of treatment packages specific to each problem which could be easily understood and within the reach of the general public.

Other ideas evolved from other people's experience. The initial ban on intercourse in order to reduce performance anxiety had been previously used by John Hunter in the 18th Century. The use of the squeeze technique for treatment of premature ejaculation evolved from the stop-start procedure of Semans and the use of a graded series of dilators in the treatment of vaginismus was earlier proposed by Shaw [24]. There are many valid criticisms of the findings of Masters and Johnson – their patients were highly selected and middle class, they were treated in special residential circumstances and their methods of assessing change were very questionable. It was impossible, however, to ignore the fact that a large number of people with sexual difficulties were being helped by a brief and directive method of treatment.

A largely pragmatic approach with its origins in the behavioural method of Masters and Johnson has been adopted in various ways to provide the main source of sex therapy within the National Health Service and the private sector in the United Kingdom. In the 1970s, this approach was also taken up by the National Marriage Guidance Council. Many modifications have been incorporated and there has been a cross-fertilisation of ideas between therapists from different backgrounds, resulting in remarkable reconciliation betwen the psychodynamic and behavioural schools. Most notable in contributing to this are Balint [30], Kaplan [4], Crown and D'Ardenne [32], and Bancroft [5]. Kaplan in particular produced a wealth of clinical evidence to show that many patients can now respond rapidly and favourably to brief forms of intervention. She proposed that the initial focus should be on the 'immediate causes' using behavioural methods and if progress is not made, then attention should change to more 'remote' causes with use of a psychodynamically orientated programme. Other methods including mastur-bation training were added later by LoPiccolo and Lobitz [33]. Other techniques of counselling and psychotherapy may be used in sexual behaviour modification [34,35]. Ellis's cognitive approach [36] emphasised the psycho-educational aspects of therapy. However, there is now a surprising level of agreement amongst most practitioners and although a considerable variation in emphasis exists, most therapists follow a modified Masters and Johnson programme.

Two major differences exist between the sex therapy model of Masters and Johnson and the modified forms in current use:

1. *Co-therapy*

Masters and Johnson strongly advocated the use of two therapists, but because of limited resources, this has not been taken up by therapists in this country except for training purposes. Masters and Johnson recommended this approach because it enabled both male and female points of view to be represented, collusion with one partner avoided, and more objectivity to be possible. A study by Mathews et al. [37] showed weak evidence to support the co-therapist approach but subsequent studies have failed to show any difference in outcome between one or two therapists [38,39]. The picture, however, is not clear and more research is needed to identify couples for whom the co-therapy approach might be beneficial.

Criteria for choosing between the concentrated daily sessions of the Masters and Johnson intensive programme and the 10-12 sessions spread over several months used by most people in this country remain to be established. The successes of Masters and Johnson in the USA have never been achieved elsewhere but, in any case, it is not practicable to use their intensive format in a non-private setting. The results of two studies support the use of less frequent sessions. Heiman and Lopiccolo [40] indicated that weekly sessions were more effective than daily sessions with problems of erectile dysfunction or secondary orgasmic dysfunction. Mathews et al. [41] found that women with impaired sexual interest appeared to benefit more from weekly rather than monthly sessions, whereas the men preferred monthly contact. Tentative conclusions might be drawn that weekly sessions are desirable in the early stages of treatment, but longer spacing may be used as treatment proceeds and progress is being made.

2. General Counselling

It is now recognised that the problems related to human sexuality are so varied that they require a broad spectrum of help. The factors which determine whether help is sought are complex and noticeable differences have been observed in the ways in which men and women present their difficulties. Men most often complain of performance problems, women complain of the subjective quality of the sexual experience. Sexual problems vary in presentation, the nature of their severity and the effects on the people concerned. The individual's acceptance of his or her sexual feelings, the relationship between partners and the relevance of physical or medical factors must all be considered.

It is important that social workers and the wide range of health professionals recognise that many sexual difficulties can be helped within the context of a general counselling relationship, do not require specialised help and can even be distorted by referral to specialised agencies.

a. Many of these difficulties can respond well to *increased reassurance and understanding* plus *information* and *education*. Providing information about male and female anatomy, forms of foreplay and intercourse, and the male and female response cycle, can dispel myths and create realistic expectations. The use of specially prepared information sheets [42] can provide additional help. People who are disabled physically or mentally or physically ill may need specialised information.

b. Many sexual difficulties disappear when people are encouraged to talk in a relaxed way and are *given permission* to be sexual and to experiment with different ways of love-making. In other cases, permission-giving may enable couples or individuals to relinquish longstanding negative attitudes.

c. Many sexual difficulties are resolved as the couple's relationship and patterns of communication improve. Teaching the following *basic principles of communication* can often prove an effective way of enabling couples to ease their sexual tension or difficulties [42].

> Learn to communicate as adults;
> Express yourself clearly in 'I' statements;
> Listen to your partner;
> Use the skills of negotiation;
> Use praise and encouragement.

Although commonsense and clinical experience confirm the value of this kind of approach to selected problems, there is, as yet, no research evidence to confirm its effectiveness.

PRINCIPLES AND METHODS OF SEXUAL COUNSELLING

Some sexual problems are more complex and require more specialised help. There are now many agencies which specialise in the treatment of sexual problems, but unfortunately they are unevenly distributed around the country. Sexual problems clinics exist in many psychiatric hospitals staffed by specially trained psychiatrists, social workers, clinical psychologists and nurses. Some family planning clinics provide this kind of help. Some marriage guidance counsellors are trained in sex therapy methods.

The main aim of sexual counselling is to improve sexual functioning, although indirectly it may also improve the couples' general relationship and communication. The aims of sexual counselling are broadly defined by Bancroft [5] as:

1. Helping the individual to accept and feel comfortable with his or her own sexuality.

2. Helping the individual to initiate and maintain a sexual relationship.

3. Helping the couple to improve the quality of their sexual relationship.

The emphasis is on emotional attitudes and the nature of the sexual interaction, rather than sexual responses. Usually the problems that have to be tackled involve anxieties and concerns about sexuality or problems within the relationship relating to communication, unresolved resentment or lack of trust. When physical factors are involved the approach is basically the same, though in these circumstances the objective is to experience the most enjoyable sexual relationship within the limits set by the physical disability. Other therapists define much more specific goals, i.e. becoming orgasmic or delaying ejaculation, and this is an area which remains controversial.

The methods used by most sex therapists are derived from Masters and Johnson but with a greater emphasis on the psychological components; this is a good example of what Mackay [43] calls behavioural psychotherapy. The principles can be summarised as follows:

1. The client (or couple) is given some clearly defined task to do.

2. When next seen by the counsellor, the attempts to carry it out are enquired about in some detail.

3. In this way the difficulties, obstacles or resistances in carrying out such behaviour are identified.

4. The counsellor does what is necessary to resolve those difficulties.

5. The next appropriate behavioural tasks are assigned.

By imposing limits on the couple's degree of physical contact and putting a ban on intercourse, and by the setting of appropriate tasks, it is now believed that in many cases performance pressures and fear of failure can be removed. Bancroft [5] gives a clear account of this method and identifies three main components: *behavioural, educational* and *psychotherapeutic*. Important emphasis throughout is laid on the principles of communication, taking responsibility for one's sexuality and oneself, and taking responsibility for change.

1. *The behavioural component* involves setting couples a series of assignments which involve mutual touching (called sensate focus), while agreeing to keep within certain limits. The combination of specified tasks and agreed limits is expected to have a variety of effects – reduce performance anxiety, improve sexual responsiveness, check levels of trust, improve communication, identify a range of intrapersonal problems, e.g.. guilt, loss of control, fear, and interpersonal difficulties such as anger and resentment. Each person is encouraged to take responsibility for his or her own sexuality and to be more sensitive to the needs of the partner.

2. *The educational component.* Providing information when appropriate

about physical and anatomical aspects of sex with the help of diagrams and pictures is an important component, especially to ensure that the sexual response cycle is fully understood and that the couple understand why progress is made, so that they can apply the same principles if problems arise in the future. In a proportion of cases, the setting of agreed limits and appropriate behavioural goals, the provision of basic information, and instruction about the basic principles of communication may so reduce performance anxiety that normal sexual responses return quite quickly.

3. *The psychotherapeutic component.* In other cases difficulties are encountered in carrying out the behavioural tasks; helping people confront and understand these obstacles requires particular psychotherapeutic skills and is really the essence of the therapeutic process. The difficulties that hinder progress are obviously varied but certain themes commonly occur – misunderstandings about treatment aims, ignorance and incorrect explanations about sex, negative sexual attitudes and problems in relationships. The challenge at this stage is to facilitate understanding and help the person or couple resolve the difficulties that have arisen by a range of therapeutic strategies. As therapy proceeds, it is important that the responsibility for control is gradually handed back to the couple so that by the time the treatment ends, they should have experience of setting their own limits and using their initiative to cope with any setbacks. A variety of specific techniques for specific problems like vaginismus, premature ejaculation or orgasmic dysfunction can be added to the general programme. Detailed accounts of these can be found in Masters and Johnson [2], Kaplan [4] and LoPiccolo and LoPiccolo [44].

Homosexuals and homosexual couples may also have sexual difficulties and require help. Until recently such help was hard to find, or concealed within the homosexual community.

There are various differences in the types of sexual problems and sexual pressures that are experienced in homosexual relationships. Common problems can be considered under four headings:

1. Guilt about homosexual feelings;
2. Problems in forming or maintaining a close intimate relationship with a person of the same sex;
3. Sexual difficulties;
4. Coping with the social stigma that a homosexual may encounter in our society.

Male homosexual couples commonly present with problems concerning the fidelity of one partner. To a large extent, however, the problems are similar and the approach to treatment much the same as with heterosexual couples. Masters and Johnson [45] reported good results with 84 homosexual couples. They do say, however, that homosexuals are less likely than heterosexuals to offer the level of co-operation that is needed for optimal treatment, although the reasons are not clear.

In the 1960s and 1970s, when behaviour therapists were paying more attention to attempts to alter homosexual preference, a variety of aversion procedures were used to suppress homosexual responses. These are no longer considered appropriate, not only because of their negative connotations, but also because of their lack of effectiveness compared with more positive approaches.

INDIVIDUAL THERAPY

As we have seen, much of the current emphasis is on helping *couples* with sexual problems, but increasing attention is being paid to *individuals*. A proportion of patients presenting with sexual problems have no current sexual partner; others have partners who are not willing to participate. Some may have difficulty in getting into sexual relationships. For many, the problem is an individual one of longstanding sexual inhibitions, a primary lack of sexual interest, inappropriate sexual preferences or problems of self-control which may bring the individual into conflict with the law. At the present time, at least in Britain, these are more likely to be men than women, but this may change with further shifts in sexual attitudes.

Individual treatment should be considered only if clear-cut appropriate goals can be defined. The principles of behavioural psychotherapy, already described, are just as applicable to individuals, although the set of assignments will be somewhat different. In a large proportion of cases, the goals of treatment are related to 'increasing comfort with one's body' and a self-touching and exploration approach directly comparable with the early stages of couple therapy can be used. The use of sexual aids such as vibrators may also be useful, particularly in helping women experience orgasm for the first time [33].

In the Family Planning Clinic, under the guidance of Balint [30], there has been a long tradition of treating non-consummation due to vaginismus by working with the woman on her own. Unfortunately, there is little documentation of the results or characteristics of this patient group, although Ellison [46] reported on her work more systematically. Some female sex therapists in America who work with inorgasmic women, either individually or in groups, claim that the experience of self-induced orgasm through non-couple-orientated sex therapy has such an enhancing effect on self-esteem and sexual self-image that improvement in their sexual relationship readily follows [47,48].

More difficult to help are patients who experience difficulty in initiating or maintaining a sexual relationship, but the techniques of self-touching programmes and relaxation exercises, of giving the patient the task of carefully monitoring his or her own behaviour so that a sequence of tasks can be devised, can all prove helpful. Cole [48], however, believes that sex is to do with another person and to treat sexual disorders without the active involvement of a partner is a contradiction in itself [49].

Surrogate partners have been used by some therapists to overcome this problem of individuals without partners. Masters and Johnson treated 41 of their 448 male patients using surrogates, but did not use male surrogates for female patients. They have now abandoned the use of surrogates, but in California surrogates remain relatively numerous and have formed their own professional organisation. In the UK the use of surrogates remains a controversial issue, raising complex ethical, treatment and legal issues. Cole [50,49], however, advocates the use of surrogate partners to treat a single patient as a necessity, uses both male and female surrogate partners and describes them as therapists.

Cole shares the general view that whenever appropriate it is desirable that sex therapy should focus on the need to treat the relationship. He also believes, however, that sex therapists must become increasingly innovatory if they are going to help those who do not respond to conventional couple therapy and not continue to ignore the fact that sexual and loving responses do not always co-exist happily together.

GROUP THERAPY

Until recently, most group therapy was psychoanalytically orientated but in the past ten years, other approaches to treatment have been applied in group settings. The use of groups for sexual dysfunction has increased noticeably since the early 1970s. This has reflected the general interest in sex therapy and has usually involved the basic principles of behavioural psychotherapy. O'Gorman [51] used systematic desensitisation as a group process for women with sexual unresponsiveness. Others have stressed the educational component [52,53].

The most popular format is to use groups of the same sex. Groups may contain people with a variety of forms of sexual dysfunction [54], but usually the group members have similar problems, e.g. orgasmic difficulty [47], erectile impotence [55]. Others have used groups of couples either with varied or with specific problems such as premature ejaculation [56]. O'Gorman [51] ran two parallel groups, one for dysfunctional women, the other for male partners.

A review of 36 studies on the treatment of sexual dysfunction in groups by Mills and Kilmann [57] resulted in the tentative suggestion that the group method was effective in the treatment of female orgasmic dysfunction and secondary erectile dysfunction, and that same-sex groups and groups of couples were equally effective.

There is, however, no agreement about the relative advantages of group methods over couple and individual therapy.

'As with most other forms of sex therapy we will need much more sound evidence before group methods find their proper place' [5].

IS SEX THERAPY EFFECTIVE?

There is a great variation in reported success rates for sex therapy; however, many studies can be criticised because of the biased nature of the sample, the absence of adequate follow-up, or the inadequate methodology for assessing the outcome.

Experience in the UK has seldom produced results as impressive as those claimed by Masters and Johnson in a private setting in the USA. Wright et al. [58] concluded that 'no strong claims for the overall effectiveness of the sex therapy approach are at present justified', and others have been equally critical [59,60]. There is, however, some evidence in other studies to suggest a degree of success at least in the *short term* [11,8,61,40]. It appears that there is a higher success rate with vaginismus and premature ejaculation than with erectile dysfunction, and the outcome is generally poor when the presenting problem is impaired sexual interest or where there are interpersonal problems.

Much less information, however, is available about the *long-term* outcome. In one study, in which sex therapy was compared with marital therapy and relaxation, Crowe et al. [38] found that therapeutic gains were maintained one year after the end of treatment. The rate of separation in couples whose treatment is unsuccessful is relatively high and lower among couples who had a successful outcome at the end of treatment [60]. this probably reflects the severity of interpersonal difficulties when entering the relationship rather than failure of treatment.

Hawton [27] identified certain factors which appear to have important associations with outcome, although the relationship and interaction between the different factors is not entirely clear:

1. Quality of the couple's general relationship;
2. Psychopathology;
3. Motivation, particularly of the man;
4. Duration of the sexual problems;
5. Partner's previous sexual adjustment;
6. Extent of sexual attraction between the partners;
7. Early progress in therapy.

Studies with surrogate partners led Cole [49] to emphasise the importance of partner-specific elements in eliciting good sexual responses.

> 'Sexual arousal is an important element in its own right . . . . and cannot be evoked by just reducing anxiety; . . . . .good sex may not be a necessary nor even a probable element in an otherwise good relationship; and . . . . sex may be disruptive as often as it is a cohesive force.'

He suggests that there is no intrinsic reason why sex and love should always be packaged together and asks,

> 'Is it both realistic and possible always to integrate sexual and loving feelings?'

There are many people with sexual problems for whom the sex therapy approach is unhelpful or inappropriate, but it is difficult to produce clear guidelines. The important influence that serious interpersonal difficulties can have on outcome is generally recognised. People with severe problems concerning intimacy, often with origins in highly disturbed family relationships, can also be difficult to help. Kaplan [26] noted that intensive psychotherapy aimed at exploring the nature of these early relationships may be a more suitable approach for appropriate people. Factors which might suggest a poor outcome for a couple are a poor general relationship, poor motivation, current psychiatric disorder, alcoholism, physical illness, current infidelity. When such factors are identified in initial assessment it is often inadvisable to embark on therapy.

Studies that have compared the effectiveness of sex therapy with that of other forms of treatment, e.g. self-help instruction with limited therapist contact, and systematic desensitisation with counselling, have produced supportive evidence for the effectiveness of the sex therapy approach [37].

Most controlled studies have now demonstrated that:

1. Sex therapy is superior to other forms of treatment.
2. It can be effective in the short term.
3. Treatment by a single therapist is as effective as that provided by two therapists.
4. A weekly treatment programme is better than more intensive treatment.
5. Self-help treatments can make an effective contribution to couples with straightforward problems but are often insufficient on their own and require brief and regular contact with the therapist.
6. The effectiveness of sex therapy varies according to the nature of the presenting problem.

It remains unclear whether the use of a male or female therapist is more effective in particular cases. LoPiccolo found that couples in which male partners had the presenting problem did less well with a single female therapist but the reverse did not apply (cited in Bancroft [5]). In other cases, it appears that one partner might benefit from receiving special understanding from a therapist of the same sex [62].

It is generally acknowledged that the long-term results of sex therapy have not been adequately investigated and that there is still a lack of good long-term follow-up data on the effectiveness of sex therapy.

> 'We do not, however, have to conclude that sexual problems are all difficult to treat. It is now established that some are easily helped whilst others are more difficult because of intrapersonal or inter-personal difficulties. Some are complicated by physical factors not always easy to recognise; some are difficult because they are in generally poor relationships' [5].

RELATIONSHIPS BETWEEN MARITAL AND SEXUAL PROBLEMS

Sexual difficulties need not necessarily cause general marital disharmony and dissatisfaction. But it is clear that in many cases, couples with sexual problems do have unhappy marriages, and that in this respect many couples who seek sex therapy resemble the couples who seek marital therapy [28,29]. In a proportion of cases, the final outcome will be marital breakdown and divorce. Thornes and Collard [63] demonstrated that sexual dissatisfaction at the start of a marriage is associated with increased risk of the marriage ending in divorce. Watson and Brockman [60] have commented on the frequency of more general marital problems occurring in those requesting help for sexual difficulties and suggest that sex therapy for some couples is often only a final attempt to avert the inevitable marital breakdown.

Crowe [64] found that couples with general marital problems showed more improvement in their sexual relationship when specific sexual behaviour assignments were included in marital therapy. In a further study [38] he made a comparison between specific behavioural sex therapy and a less specific systems/marital approach and concluded that there was little difference in outcome between the two methods – the sex therapy group showed significantly more increase in libido at the end of treatment, but the difference was no longer apparent at follow-up.

Sager [65] discusses the complex relationship between different forms and degrees of marital disharmony and sexual dysfunction and gives some pointers to the range of situations in which the sex therapy model, with its specific goal-directed form of treatment, can and cannot be used effectively and when it is more appropriate to pursue a therapeutic programme of broader marital or individual therapy. It is often assumed that there should be a clear division between sexual and marital problems and hence between sexual or marital therapy. But there are many instances when an improvement in the sexual relationship will follow an improvement in other areas of the relationship and vice versa. Bancroft says that concerns about making the right choice between sex therapy and marital therapy are often exaggerated – 'Concentrating on the sexual part of the relationship allows a manageable focus, whilst, at the same time, dealing with issues of broader relevance' [66]. Often there are crucial problems of unresolved anger, insecurity or poor communication within the relationship; or couples express such anger or ambivalence about continuing the relationship that it is inappropriate to focus on the sexual aspects initially. In these cases, it is important that the sexual and non-sexual components can be dealt with by the same therapist within the same course of counselling.

CONCLUSION

In the rest of this article I shall highlight four areas of importance in the development of services for sex therapy in the UK:

1. Training;
2. Provision of services;
3. Prevention of sexual problems;
4. Further research.

1. *Training*

Sex therapy services and training have developed in a rather haphazard way in the UK. The place of sex therapy in medicine remains unclear and the provision of specialised clinics is in the main dependent on the enthusiasm of individuals rather than it being an integral part of Health Service policy. The National Marriage Guidance Council has devised its own training programme and some marriage guidance counsellors are now trained to help couples with sexual problems as well as with general relationship problems [67]. The introduction of training to the medical curriculum and to social work courses has developed much more slowly and, in the field of social work in particular, neither formal social work training nor the present levels of supervision and consultancy provide social workers with sufficient skills, knowledge and understanding to enable them to work confidently and competently across this broad field of practice [68].

Many couples and individuals in a wide variety of settings who seek help for sexual difficulties do not require sex therapy but can benefit from brief counselling and information. Social workers, in particular, must be prepared to work effectively with a whole range of sexual and marital problems and sexually related anxieties. They must find ways of responding more creatively to the sexual needs of handicapped people and be able to facilitate the healthy sexual development of young people in residential care. They must develop a more enlightened response to both sexual abuse and sexual offences and find more effective ways of working with these difficulties. Much more training is needed to help them gain insight into their own sexual feelings, develop a body of knowledge and understanding about sex and sexuality, learn a wider range of basic techniques for helping, and increase their ability to put people at their ease when talking about sexual matters.

2. Provision of Services

Provision of services in the UK at present is patchy. It is clear that there is a need to extend the present services to cover the whole country more adequately. However, there are also special groups of people who might benefit but for whom such help is rarely available. Clinical experience has shown that sex therapy with people with *physical disability* is often very fruitful and, in many instances, can be briefer than therapy with people whose problems are entirely emotional or interpersonal in origin. Very often there is reluctance to explore the sexuality of disabled people [69,70,71]. Another equally important area of need lies with the *mentally handicapped*, another large group of people whose sexual difficulties have hardly been explored.

3. Prevention of Sexual Problems

There is little doubt that inadequate sexual knowledge is an important factor in the aetiology of many sexual problems. Many people have had little or no sex education. In dealing with people's sexual difficulties and relationships it is often apparent that if people had only known the facts, understood their feelings and had healthier attitudes towards sexuality, much unhappiness could have been avoided. Sex education, however, still remains a controversial issue, with many feeling that sex education is the prerogative of parents. Schofield [20] found in 1965 that only 27 per cent of young people in England had received any sex education from their mothers; and fathers played no part at all. Farrell [21] found that 96 per cent of parents agreed with sex education for their children at school, but when permission is sought to provide sex education there was likely to be opposition from parents who have difficulties with their own sexuality and are least able to provide this teaching at home.

Schofield [72] looked at the teenagers he had studied seven years before to see what effects sex education had had. He concluded that their attitudes had changed but not their behaviour; attitudes change slowly – putting these attitudes into practice takes even longer. Changes *are* taking place, values are changing, but many of our social values and attitudes towards sexuality remain hypocritical, dishonest or distorted. Myths need to be challenged, social attitudes need to change, destructive effects and irresponsible views need to be minimised. Books have a part to play in encouraging responsible attitudes, e.g. *Our Bodies Ourselves* [73], *Treat Yourself to Sex* [74] and

Coping with Sexual Relationships [75]. Much more needs to be done within the family, the schools and other settings to help people break the cycle of negative learning about sex and the denial by the individual of his sexuality; and to enable them to develop healthy, informed and compassionate attitudes towards sexuality and relationships.

4. Further Research

It is generally recognised that more research and investigation is required in several aspects of sexual therapy. These include:

(1) Long-term outcomes.
(2) Refusals, early drop outs, and the high proportion of people who fail to attend for first appointment.
(3) Approaches to treatment and different types of client – with few exceptions, the precise type of sexual dysfunction tells us little about the most effective approach to treatment or the problems we are likely to encounter.
(4) Greater precision in assessment of people for sex therapy or other forms of therapy.
(5) Finally, it should be recognised that the approaches outlined in this paper have been developed in the context of contemporary western societies.

The basic values underlying the sex therapy model assume an egalitarian reciprocal relationship between men and women, with an emphasis on the value of open communication and mutual sexual pleasure. The relevance of current sex therapy practice for societies with radically different social and sexual expectations remains uncertain, and the question should be approached with caution and sensitivity. The dangers of imposing unacceptable sexual values on people is obvious. Even within our own society, there may be groups and subcultures where these liberal values are not fully shared and appropriate modifications may be required.

References

1. Masters, W.H. & Johnson, V.E. *Human Sexual Response*. J. & A. Churchill, London, 1966.
2. Masters, W.H. & Johnson, V.E. *Human Sexual Inadequacy*. J. & A. Churchill, London, 1970.

3. Belliveau, F. & Richter, L. *Understanding Human Sexual Inadequacy*. Hodder and Stoughton, London, 1971.

4. Kaplan, H.S. *The New Sex Therapy*. Bailliere Tindall, London, 1974 (also published by Penguin).

5. Bancroft, J. *Human Sexuality and Its Problems*. Churchill Livingstone, Edinburgh, 1983.

6. Rusbridger, A. *A Concise History of the Sex Manual 1886-1986*. Faber and Faber, London, 1986.

7. Zilbergeld, B. *Men and Sex*. Fontana, London, 1980.

8. Bancroft, J. & Coles, L. 'Three Years Experience in a Sexual Problems Clinic' *British Medical Journal*. 1, 1976, 1575-1577.

9. Rainwater, L. 'Some Aspects of Lower Class Sexual Behaviour' *Journal of Social Issues*. 22, 1966, 96-108.

10. Begg, A., Dickerson, M. & Loudon, N.B. 'Frequency of Self-Reporting Sexual Problems in a Family Planning Clinic' *Journal of Family Planning Doctors*. 2, 1976, 41-48.

11. Hawton, K. 'The Behavioural Treatment of Sexual Dysfunction' *British Journal of Psychiatry*. 140, 1982, 94-101.

12. Brown, P.T. 'The Development of Sexual Function Therapies After Masters and Johnson'. In Armytage, W.H.G., Chester, R., & Pool, J. (Eds.) *Changing Patterns in Sexual Behaviour*. Academic Press, London, 1980.

13. Brown, P.T. & Riley, A.J. 'Editorial' *Sexual and Marital Therapy*. 1, 1986, 3-6.

14. Freud, S. *Three Essays on the Theory of Sexuality*. Hogarth Press, London, 1905.

15. Erikson, E.H. *Childhood and Society*. Penguin, Harmondsworth, 1965.

16. Freud, A. *Normality and Pathology in Childhood*. International Universities Press, New York, 1965.

17. Kinsey, A.C., Pomeroy, W.B. & Martin, C.E. *Sexual Behaviour in the Human Male*. Saunders, Philadelphia, 1948.

18. Kinsey, A.C., Pomeroy, W.B., Martin, C.E. & Gebhard, P.H. *Sexual Behaviour in the Human Female*. Saunders, Philadelphia, 1953.

19. Gebhard, P.H. & Johnson, A.B. *The Kinsey Data*. Saunders, Philadelphia, 1979.

20. Schofield, M. *The Sexual Behaviour of Young People*. Longmans, London, 1965.

21. Farrell, C. *My Mother Said*. Routledge & Kegan Paul, London, 1978.

22. Fisher, S. *Understanding the Female Orgasm*. Penguin, Harmondsworth, 1973.

23. Hite, S. *The Hite Report: A Nationwide Study of Female Sexuality*. Dell, New York, 1976.

24. Cole, M.J. 'Sex Therapy – A Critical Appraisal' *British Journal of Psychiatry*. 147, 1985, 337-351.

25. Fairburn, C.G, Dickson, M.G. & Greenwood, J. *Sexual Problems and their Management*. Churchill Livingstone, Edinburgh, 1983.

26. Kaplan, H.S. *Disorders of Sexual Desire and Other New Concepts and Techniques in Sex Therapy*. Brunner Mazel, New York, 1979,

27. Hawton, K. *Sex Therapy: A Practical Guide*. Oxford University Press, Oxford, 1985.

28. Frank, E., Anderson, C. & Kupfer, D.J. 'Profiles of Couples Seeking Sex Therapy and Marital Therapy' *American Journal of Psychiatry*. 133, 1976, 559-562.

29. Frank, E. & Rubinstein, D. 'Frequency of Sexual Dysfunction in "Normal" Couples' *New England Journal of Medicine*. 229, 1978, 111-115.

30. Balint, M. *The Doctor, His Patient and the Illness*. Pitman Medical, London, 1957.

31. Tunadine, P., Morrow, C.S. & Hutchinson, F.D. 'Sex Problems in Practice. Training and Referral' *British Medical Journal*. 282, 1981, 1669-1672.

32. Crown, S. & D'Ardenne, P. 'Controversies, Methods and Results' *British Journal of Psychiatry*. 140, 1982, 70-77.

33. LoPiccolo, J. & Lobitz, W.C. 'The Role of Masturbation in the Treatment of Orgasmic Dysfunction' *Archives of Sexual Behaviour*. 2, 1972, 163-171.

34. Nelson-Jones, R. *The Theory and Practice of Counselling Psychology*. Holt, Rinehart & Winston, London, 1982.

35. Dryden, W. (Ed.) *Individual Therapy in Britain*. Harper and Row, London, 1984.

36. Ellis, A. 'Treatment of Erectile Dysfunction'. In Leiblum, S.R. & Pervin, L.A. (Eds.) *Principles and Practices of Sex Therapy*. Tavistock, London, 1980.

37. Mathews, A., Bancroft, J. & Whitehead, A. 'The Behavioural Treatment of Sexual Inadequacy: A Comparative Study' *Behaviour Research and Therapy*. 14, 1976, 427-436.

38. Crowe, M.J., Gillan, P. & Golombek, S. 'Form and Content in the Conjoint Treatment of Sexual Dysfunction: A Controlled Study' *Behaviour Research and Therapy*, 19, 1981, 47-54.

39. LoPiccolo, J., Heiman, J.R., Hogan, D.R. & Roberts, C.W. 'Effectiveness of Single Therapists Versus Cotherapy Teams in Sex Therapy' *Journal of Consulting and Clinical Psychology*. 53, 1985, 287-294.

40. Heiman, J.R. & LoPiccolo, J. 'Clinical Outcome of Sex Therapy' *Archives of General Psychiatry*. 40, 1983, 443-449.

41. Mathews, A., Whitehead, A. and Kellett, J. 'Psychological and Hormonal Factors in the Treatment of Female Sexual Dysfunction' *Psychological Medicine*. 13, 1983, 83-92.

42. Greenwood, J. & Bancroft, J. 'Counselling Notes for Couples in Sex Therapy'. In Bancroft, J. *Human Sexuality and its Problems*. Churchill Livingstone, Edinburgh, 1983, 303-313.

43. Mackay, D. 'Behavioural Psychotherapy'. In Dryden, W. (Ed.) *Individual Therapy in Britain*. Harper and Row, London, 1984.

44. LoPiccolo, J. and LoPiccolo, L. *Handbook of Sex Therapy*. Plenum Press, New York, 1978.

45. Masters, W.H. & Johnson, V.E. *Homosexuality in Perspective*. Little, Brown & Co., Boston, 1979.

46. Ellison, C. 'Psychosomatic Factors in the Unconsummated Marriage' *Journal of Psychosomatic Research*. 12, 1968, 61-66.

47. Barbach, L.G. 'Group Treatment of Pre-orgasmic Women' *Journal of Sex and Marital Therapy*. 1, 1974, 139-145.

48. Heiman, J.R., LoPiccolo, L. & LoPiccolo, J. *Becoming Orgasmic: A Sexual Growth Problem for Women*. Prentice Hall, New Jersey 1976.

49. Cole, M.J. 'Surrogate Sex Therapy'. In Dryden, W. (Ed.) *Marital Therapy in Britain Vol.2*. Harper and Row, London, 1985.

50. Cole, M.J. 'The Use of Surrogate Sex Partners in the Treatment of Sex Dysfunctions and Allied Conditions' *British Journal of Sexual Medicine*. 9, 1982, 13-20.

51. O'Gorman, E. 'The Treatment of Frigidity: A Comparative Study of Group and Individual Desensitisation' *British Journal of Psychiatry*. 132, 1978, 580-584.

52. Gillan, P., Golombok, S. & Becker, P. 'NHS Sex Therapy Groups for Women' *British Journal of Sexual Medicine*. 7, 1980, 44-47.

53. Leiblum, S.R. & Rosen, R.C. 'The Weekend Workshop for Dysfunctional Couples – Assets and Limitations' *Journal of Sex and Marital Therapy*. 5, 1979, 57-69.

54. Zilbergeld, B. 'Group Treatment of Sexual Dysfunction in Men without Partners' *Journal of Sex and Marital Therapy*. 1, 1975, 204-214.

55. Lobitz, W.C. & Baker, E.L. 'Group Treatment of Single Males with Erectile Dysfunction' *Archives of Sexual Behaviour*. 8, 1979, 127-138.

56. Kaplan, H.S., Kohl, R.N., Pomeroy, W.B., Offit, A.K. & Hogan, B. 'Group Treatment for Premature Ejaculation' *Archives of Sexual Behaviour*. 3, 1974, 443-452.

57. Mills, K.H. & Kilmann, P.R. 'Group Treatment of Sexual Dysfunctions: A Methodological Review of the Outcome Literature' *Journal of Sex and Marital Therapy*. 8, 1982, 259-296.

58. Wright, J., Perreault, R. & Mathieu, M. 'The Treatment of Sexual Dysfunction – A Review' *Archives of General Psychiatry*. 34, 1977, 881-890.

59. Kilmann, P.R. & Auerbach, R. 'Treatment of Premature Ejaculation and Psychogenic Impotence: A Critical Review of the Literature' *Archives of General Psychiatry*. 8, 1979, 81-100.

60. Watson, J.P. & Brockman, B. 'A Follow-up of Couples Attending a Psychosexual Problems Clinic' *British Journal of Clinical Psychology*. 21, 1982, 143-144.

61. Duddle, C.M. 'The Treatment of Marital Psycho-Sexual Problems' *British Journal of Psychiatry*. 127, 1975, 169-170.

62. Arentewicz, G. & Schmidt, G. (Eds.) *The Treatment of Sexual Disorders*. Basic Books, New York, 1983.

63. Thornes, B. & Collard, J. *Who Divorces?* Routledge & Kegan Paul, London, 1979.

64. Crowe, M.J. 'Conjoint Marital Therapy: A Controlled Outcome Study' *Psychological Medicine*. 8, 1978, 623-626.

65. Sager, C.J. 'Sexual Dysfunctions and Marital Discord'. In Kaplan, H.S. *The New Sex Therapy*. Bailliere Tindall, London, 1974 (chapter 24).

66. Bancroft, J. 'Marital Sex Therapy'. In Dryden, W. (Ed.) *Marital Therapy in Britain Vol.2*. Harper and Row, London, 1985.

67. Heisler, J. *Sexual Therapy in the National Marriage Guidance Council*. Marriage Guidance Council, Rugby, 1983.

68. Davis, L. *Sex and the Social Worker*. Heinemann, London, 1983.

69. Heslinga, K. *Not Made of Stone*. Thomas, Illinois, 1974.

70. Greengross, W. *Entitled to Love: The Sexual and Emotional Needs of the Handicapped*. Mallerby Press and National Marriage Guidance Council, in association with the National Fund for Research into Crippling Diseases, London, 1976.

71. Steward, W.F.R. 'Sexual Fulfilment for the Handicapped' *British Journal of Hospital Medicine*. 20, 1978, 676-680.

72. Schofield, M. *The Sexual Behaviour of Young Adults*. Longmans, London, 1973.

73. Phillips, A. and Rakusen, J. *Our Bodies, Ourselves*. Boston Women's Health Collective, Boston, 1978. (Also published by Penguin).

74. Brown, P. & Faulder, C. *Treat Yourself to Sex: A Guide for Good Loving*. Dent, London, 1977. (Also published by Penguin).

75. Greenwood, J. *Coping with Sexual Relationships*. Macdonald, Edinburgh, 1984.

Support for Women Who Have Been Raped

Siobhan Lloyd

INTRODUCTION

Research on the subject of rape and other forms of violence against women has grown in recent years. Not only has it become less of a taboo subject since the mid-1970s but, with the growth of rape crisis centres in Britain and the United States, new approaches to giving support for women who have experienced sexual violence have developed. It is also becoming apparent that changes are occurring in the way police question complainers of rape, and it may be that some of these changes are attributable both to changing public attitudes towards the crime of rape and to pressures from the women's movement.

This article reviews the evidence on the incidence of rape and sexual assault; it summarises some of the main research findings on the effects of rape on a woman, and it presents one example of the way in which women themselves have created resources for supporting women who have been sexually assaulted by a stranger or a trusted adult. Reference is also made to recent changes in police practice in cases where a rape is alleged. Although the article confines itself in the main to material on adult women who have been raped, some reference is also made to support for women who were sexually abused as children. The article does not analyse the legal context for the crime of rape, nor does it go into great detail about the criminal procedure following an arrest for the crime.

THE INCIDENCE OF RAPE – HOW COMMON IS IT?

Over the last decade there has been increasing public concern about the difficulties faced by women who report incidents of rape or sexual assault to the police. Rape is a vastly under-reported crime. Dukes and Mattley [1] estimate that 75 per cent of rapes in the United States were unreported and the recent British Crime Survey [2] found that only 7 per cent of incidents of sexual assault uncovered by the police in Scotland were reported to the police. Evidence from rape crisis centres also suggests that rape is greatly under-reported. London rape crisis centre reports [3] note that 25 per cent of women who use the service have contacted the police. Edinburgh Rape Crisis Centre figures, for a sample of fifty consecutive calls, show that 56 per cent had reported the rape [4] and Birmingham Rape Crisis Centre noted a 39.8 per cent reporting rate in 1980 [6]. The sources of these figures do not reveal whether contact with rape crisis centres took place before or after the incidents had been reported to the police. In Aberdeen, only 4 per cent of all callers between 1982 and 1986 had contacted the police before getting in touch with the rape crisis centre.

A community-based study of violence against women in Leeds, carried out in 1981 [7] acknowledged that women are more likely to report violent incidents 'When the aggressor is a stranger and less likely when he is known.' The researchers concluded that women suppress information concerning violence to them for a variety of reasons:

> 'They may not want to remember a painful situation, or may not want the story to spread further.'

The researchers go further when they argue:

> 'Victim blaming shows that our culture holds women responsible for the violent behaviour of men, and this increases with the closeness of the relationship. It is not surprising that women as well as men comply with this dominant cultural value . . . .'

In 1982, a survey on the incidence of rape and sexual assault in London was carried out by Women Against Rape, a campaigning organisation run for and by women [8]. A total of 1,236 completed questionnaires were returned, and showed that one in six (17 per cent) of respondents had been raped and one in three (31 per cent) had been sexually assaulted. Only 5 per cent of the women who were raped or sexually assaulted by a man known to them reported the incident to the police, and the figure for reported assault by a stranger was 31 per cent.

Despite the figures reported above, the incidence of reported rapes has shown an increase on both sides of the Atlantic in recent years. It is not clear, however, whether the increase is the result of an increase in reporting or an increase in the number of rapes being committed. Any conclusions from the figures should be made with caution.

TABLE 1

Incidence of rape in the United States and Britain

Year	Number of rapes recorded		Rate per 10,000 females	
	USA	Britain	USA	Britain
1970	37,860	893	35	3.7
1974	55,210	1094	51	4.6
1978	67,131	1225	61	5.1
1982	77,763	1334	71	5.1

Source: Blair, I. *Investigating Rape: A New Approach for Police.* Croom Helm, Dover, 1985.

The lower overall rates in Britain have been attributed to lower reporting rates and lower recidivism by rapists [9].

In addition, the rate of reporting for rape offences is lower than for other crimes and in 1982 the United States Federal Bureau of Investigation's Crime Statistics stated that rape:

> 'is still recognised as one of the most under reported of all Index Crimes' [10].

In an American study the National Opinion Research Centre (NORC) conducted a survey of 19,000 households into actual and reported rates of crime. A comparison between the rates of crime reported in the survey and officially reported rates during the same period by the Uniform Crime Reports (UCR) is given in Table 2.

TABLE 2

Comparison of actual and reported crime rates in the United States

	NORC 1965-66	UCR 1966	% reported occurring
	(Per 100,000 pop.)		
Forcible rape	42.5	12.2	28.7
Robbery	94.0	61.4	65.2
Aggravated assault	218.3	106.6	48.2

Source: *President's Commission on Law Enforcement and the Administration of Justice. The Challenge of Crime in a Free Society.* Washington, 1967, quoted in Blair [9].

Even when a rape is reported, the clear-up rate is lower than for other crimes. Chambers and Millar [10] note that 30 per cent of cases sent by the police to the Procurator Fiscal in two Scottish cities were not proceeded against. Figures on clear-up may be slightly misleading as they are attributable to the year in which the clear up occurs, which may or may not be the year in which the crime occurred. The clear-up rate does appear to be rising but it is still less than for other crimes.

TABLE 3

Clear up rates for crimes of indecency in Scotland, 1972-1984

	% recorded crimes			
	1972	1976	1980	1984
Sexual assault (including rape)	57	44	48	57
Lewd and libidinous behaviour	63	51	47	47
Other	97	100	99	99

Source: *Criminal Statistics, Scotland, 1972-1984.* Cmnd. 9403, Scottish Home and Health Department, Edinburgh, 1984.

When women decide to report an incident of rape they often have great doubts and hesitations about the wisdom of their decision. In a 1983 Scottish study which examined what happened when women reported an incident of sexual assault to the police, 62 per cent said that they had no doubts about their decision to report. Of the remainder, however, 20 per cent had some doubts about reporting and 15 per cent said they had lots of doubts [10]. A significant number of doubts related to publicity surrounding the case and confidentiality for themselves during any subsequent investigations. Hall [8] found that 75 per cent of women who did not report their rape did so because they did not expect the police to be 'on their side' in any subsequent investigations. It would appear that the principal reasons which encourage a women to report the incident are a desire for justice and a realisation that not to do so will leave the rapist free to rape another woman. The main pressures against reporting are embarrassment, fear of retaliation and fear of poor treatment by the police [9]. Katz and Mazur [11] have also suggested that a reason for under reporting is the way in which a complainant's personal and moral background is questioned by police and defence lawyers if a case goes to court.

Further barriers to reporting relate to a number of myths surrounding the crime of rape, myths which have served to perpetuate an image of the crime which is very different from reality.

RAPE – MYTH AND REALITY

The myths about rape which still persist leave many women to cope alone and unaided after the assault. For example, there is still a widely held belief that women secretly enjoy rape and that it is 'sex when they don't want it'. In reality, rape is a crime which often involves humiliation, beatings and the use of physical restraint. Studies have consistently shown that most rapes involve force to some extent and that the threat of further violence is often used to guarantee silence after the event from the woman who has been raped. Amir [12], in a study of all the rapes reported to the police in Philadelphia between 1958 and 1960, notes that physical force was used in 85 per cent of cases. Women in the study also reported that higher degrees of resistance provoked greater violent attack from the rapist. Chambers and Millar [10] report that firearms were used in 19 per cent of incidents and that 40 per cent of complainers in their sample suffered some form of physical injury during the attack. Wright [13], who examined 255 incidents of rape on police files in England, found that 32 per cent of the women suffered injury. Chambers and Millar [10] draw attention to the fact that physical injuries should not be confused with the use of physical force or violence by the rapist, since in many cases the physical force used (choking, hitting, restraint) does not result in visible physical injury.

A second myth is that rape is a crime committed by strangers, by men who are psychologically disturbed and who cannot control their sexual urges. As Toner [14] commented:

> 'The popular view is that, if the rapist cannot be labelled fiend, monster or maniac, then he probably isn't a rapist at all.'

An American probation officer working in a Californian prison described rapists with whom he was in contact as follows:

> 'Those men were the most normal in there. They had a lot of hang ups, but they were the same sort of hang ups as men working out on the streets' [15].

Amir, after extensive research of 646 rape cases concluded that the majority of convicted rapists in his sample had 'a normal sexual personality' [12]. Indeed only 2-3 per cent of convicted rapists in Britain have been assessed as being in need of psychiatric treatment [16].

TABLE 4
Disposals for persons with charge proved in Scotland, 1984

	Absolute Discharge	Caution/ Admonish	Probation	CSO	Fine	Prison	Y.O.I.	Detention	Hospital Order Insanity
Sexual assault[1]	–	15	21	4	37	10	4	2	
Lewd and libidinous[2] behaviour	1	43	77	4	173	43	1	3	0
Other sexual crimes[3]	1	74	22	5	1165	17	3	1	0

Source: Scottish Criminal Statistics, 1984. Scottish Home and Health Department, Edinburgh, 1986.

1. Comprises rape, assault with intent to rape and indecent assault.
2. Comprises lewd and libidinous practices and indecent exposure.
3. Includes prostitution.

An indication of the extent of psychological disturbance among rapists can be gained from examining the number of convicted rapists who were declared mentally ill. Scottish statistics for one sample year are given in Table 4.

The effect of this myth on women is to make them believe that they will recognise a rapist and avoid him. It also gives an illusion of safety, and minimises the possibility for 'normal men' whom women know and trust of being rapists. Hall [8] notes that three out of every four women who admitted having been raped in the W.A.R. survey knew their assailant. Sixteen per cent were known acquaintances, ten per cent were partners or former partners, eight per cent were friends or workmates, eight per cent were close family members, four per cent were husbands, three per cent were neighbours and three per cent were known to the woman in another capacity.

The location in which rapes occur provides further evidence that many women are raped by men whom they trust or know well enough to let them into their homes. Amir [12] noted that 46 per cent of the cases in his sample were raped at the home of the rapist or of the woman. Eighteen per cent occurred outdoors and 15 per cent took place in cars. Chambers and Millar [10] report slightly different findings, with 52 per cent of the rapes in their sample occurring out of doors (including a common stair, close or alleyway into a tenement building). Thirty-three per cent of their sample were raped in the woman's or rapist's home. They conclude that, after public parks and open spaces, the complainer is most vulnerable in her own home.

There are a number of studies which have shown the extent to which the rape is a premeditated event. Amir, for example, concludes that 70 per cent of the cases in his study were planned before the event, 11 per cent were partially planned and 11 per cent were 'impulse crimes' [12].

Not only is it a common assumption that rape is committed by certain types of men, but also against certain types of women. It is commonly believed, for example, that prostitutes cannot be raped since they openly engage in sexual activity, choosing where and when to have sexual intercourse. This assumption is totally unfounded, since choosing to engage in sexual activity does not mean choosing to be raped.

Women often derive a sense of security from the misconception that ugly, fat or old women are not raped. Figures from London Rape Crisis Centre show that although 70 per cent of women who contacted the centre were aged between 16 and 35 years of age at the time of their assault, eight per cent were over 35 and 22 per cent were less than 15 years old.

A further myth is that women 'ask for it' or that they provoke a sexual attack. Comments which refer to a woman's clothing, her 'unfeminine' behaviour, her confidence or assertiveness result in rape being regarded in this instance as 'punishment' for inappropriate female behaviour. Wright [13] concluded that:

> 'a tiny proportion (less than 4 per cent) of cases involved some vulnerability in the victim – she may have agreed initially to sexual intercourse, for example, and changed her mind at the last moment – but even these incidents are not "victim precipitated".'

Barbara Toner confirms this view:

> 'There is no evidence to suggest that rape victims are endowed with any physical or psychological features which make them targets for the crime' [14].

Furthermore, women are often disbelieved when they report a rape. This results from the myth that women are prone to making false allegations of rape. In one celebrated case in 1976, Judge Sutcliffe was quoted as saying to a jury at the Old Bailey before they retired to consider their verdict in a rape trial,

> 'It is well know that women in particular, and small boys, are liable to be untruthful and to invent stories' [17]

In 1970 the New York City Police Force carried out an investigation into this issue, and concluded that false allegations of rape amounted to only two per cent – a figure similar to other crimes [18].

The final misconception to address is the labelling of rape as a sexual crime. Time and time again women report to Rape Crisis Centres an assault in which they have been subjected to physical and emotional abuse. Rape is not experienced by women as a sexual act but as a threat to life. Amir [12] concludes that the only difference between men who chose to rape and those who did not was that rapists had a greater tendency to express violence and rage. Brownmillar [19] concludes that rape was an act of plunder and Groth [20], in his study of convicted rapists, found that the men themselves did not view their crime as being primarily of a sexual nature. He states:

> 'Rape is a pseudo-sexual act, a pattern of sexual behaviour that is

concerned much more with status, hostility, control and dominance than with pleasure or sexual satisfaction. It is sexual behaviour in the primary service of non-sexual needs.'

Groth's research confirms the testimony of women themselves, and it is reinforced by Blair [9] who notes:

'Although the violation of rape concerns the sexual organs and it involves sexual taboos, many victims view the crime asexually, and respond to it as a life threatening situation.'

This view is further elaborted by Burgess and Holstrom [21] who conclude:

'Rape is not primarily a sexual act. . . . rape is primarily an act of violence with sex as the weapon.'

The importance of analysing the myths referred to above is that they have been responsible for perpetuating assumptions about women's behaviour in relation to men, and have served to create a legacy of guilt, self-blame and powerlessness to many women who have experienced sexual assault.

WOMEN'S REACTIONS TO RAPE

When a woman has been raped she has to overcome the barriers of silence which have been responsible for the prevention of recognition of this serious social problem. She also has to subject herself, if she reports the crime, to situations in which she will be forced to relive the experience. These situations include taking a statement at the police station, a forensic medical examination and, if the case goes to court, close cross-questioning by the defence lawyer. The London rape crisis centre [22] acknowledges that 'there is no right or wrong way to react to sexual violence.' The myths which were outlined earlier have been a powerful influence in confirming a woman's experience of guilt, self-blame and loss of control. Each woman has her own individual way of reacting to rape, but some of the more common reactions are outlined below.

Many women experience some degree of shock which may manifest itself either in complete calm and apparent lack of emotion, or in laughing or crying hysterically or an inability to think clearly. Another common reaction is to feel loss of control. Since rape is a violation of a woman's self-esteem, she often feels that she has no subsequent control over anything in her life. Small decisions become hard to make and a woman's sense of powerlessness can be heightened if she has reported the rape to the police.

Women often experience nightmares which can take the form of specific and detailed images of the rape or vague and difficult to articulate feelings. Fear is another recurring reaction, ranging from paralysing terror when the event is recalled, to fear of an event or situation which reminds the woman of her rape. Shame is also common. Many women feel dirty and spend time washing themselves over and over again in order to feel clean. At the other end of the spectrum some women react by *not* cleaning themselves, feeling that they are no longer worth any effort. It is important to acknowledge such feelings as a normal manifestation of the fact that a woman's body has been used without her consent.

Guilt is the most common reaction to rape, and many women feel guilty to some extent for what has happened. She will always be able to think of something which could have been done to stop the attack. The list of 'if onlys' is endless. Often a woman's unfounded guilt is exacerbated by the police and legal system implying that the rape is the woman's fault with questions like 'Why didn't you lock your door?' or 'Why did you accept the lift?'. It is hardly surprising, therefore, that many women believe themselves to be as guilty as the men who raped them.

Another important and common reaction to rape is physical revulsion. Women report not being able to touch or be touched by people close to them. This is particularly common with women who have reported a rape and who have had to endure a medical examination, usually performed by a male police surgeon. Women also report difficulties with male sexual relationships after a rape. Vaginismus is a common reaction and often women react by either rejecting any sexual contact with men, or by engaging in sexual activity with many partners. The latter is a reaction to low self-esteem, to feeling worthless and to feeling that one's body has no right to be protected. The former reaction is a control response whereby women seek protection from potentially violent male actions.

Two further emotions – anger and depression – are commonplace and closely linked. Women who have been raped often do not show any overt expression of anger to what has happened to them. This is because they have accepted total responsibility for the crime which has been committed against them. Any anger which is experienced by the woman often tends to be misplaced inwards or suppressed, resulting in depression.

RAPE TRAUMA SYNDROME

One of the most helpful discoveries in understanding women's reactions to rape was the identification of rape trauma syndrome by Burgess and Holstrom in 1974 [21]. Early work by Lindemann [23] developed into an area of study known as 'crisis theory'. Lindemann asserted that human reaction to crisis is predictable and often displays common features of extreme suggestibility and helplessness after the event. Reactions often depend on the perceived severity of the crisis and the social resilience of the abused person.

Since rape can be defined as a severe crisis, these reactions can also be expected in women who have suffered this form of abuse. Burgess and Holstrom set out in the 1970s to examine the possibility that women who have been raped might experience symptoms particular to their experience. Their study was based on a sample of 140 women aged between 17 and 70 and from all social classes who had been raped and who presented at a Boston hospital during a twelve month period. There was also a five-year follow-up. They concluded that there were two phases in a woman's reaction to rape. In the first few hours or days following an attack women experienced an acute sense of disbelief and shock, compounded by physical trauma associated with the violence used. They also experienced feelings of fear, humiliation and embarrassment, anger, desire for revenge and self blame.

Interestingly, the researchers also discovered that women responded in almost equal proportions with hysterical crying, laughing or 'silent composure'. This phase was followed by a period of 'integration and resolution' when the women tried to come to terms with what had happened to them. The researchers noted that during this phase women often changed their address, job or circle of friends. They also commonly expressed disbelief at what had happened and were determined to 'carry on as normal'. Difficulties in close relationships were apparent and women reported recurrent nightmares and phobias.

Burgess and Holstrom argued that although victims of serious crime all suffer from unpleasant reactions, the symptoms displayed by women who have been raped are both more severe and predictable. They suggested that this is because:

> 'normal crisis reactions are compounded by the taboos surrounding sexuality and the conflict generated by the mythology surrounding rape, so that guilt, shame and self-blame keep emerging.'

Basuk [24] goes further and identifies four stages of rape trauma syndrome, namely threat, impact, recoil and reconstitutive phases. During the threat phase the woman may attempt to escape from the rapist if she is not paralysed with terror. She may verbally or physically try to prevent the rape or may have resigned herself to it and retreats into herself in an attempt to disassociate herself from the experience. After the impact stage the woman enters the recoil phase when she may try to deny her experience by resuming her life as if nothing has happened. Some women impose restrictions on their activities through fear of further attack or as the result of diminished self-esteem. In the final stage of recovery, the reconstitutive phase, the woman is more able to deal with specific issues which the assault has raised for her. These issues, Basuk argues, will be determined by conflicts re-evoked by the rape and life-stage developmental issues. Once again symptoms such as depression, anxiety or phobias may emerge.

Weis and Borges [25] have suggested that the decision to report a rape can also become part of the trauma. This has obvious implications for the way in which police respond to a complaint of rape at both the immediate stage of police questioning and later if the case comes to court. Burgess and Holstrom [21] argue that:

> 'the manner in which they are treated by police as a consequence of that decision (i.e. to report the crime) will have a major impact on the severity of the trauma they may suffer.'

They also suggest that the ability of a woman to overcome the trauma depends on three factors; her personal stability, support from her personal network and the manner in which she is treated if the case goes to court.

The identification of rape trauma syndrome, which is now part of accepted evidence in American rape trials [26] has also given viability to the special treatment of women by the criminal justice system and it has also contributed to the setting up of rape crisis centres in the United States and Britain.

THE WORK OF RAPE CRISIS CENTRES

In Britain there is no official provision for the support and aftercare of women who have experienced rape or sexual assault. In 1976, however, Britain's first rape crisis centre opened in London. By 1986 there were 47 such centres operating throughout England, Wales, Scotland and Northern Ireland. Scotland has seven centres. Only two centres, in London and Birmingham, offer a 24 hour service. The remainder offer telephone support on a limited basis and they also meet women to offer ongoing support. Rape crisis centres are run largely on a voluntary basis, by women for women, and they are usually organised along collective lines, with decisions and responsibilities shared between members. They also offer medical and legal advice on all aspects of sexual abuse, and members will accompany women to the police if they decide to adopt that course of action. Some centres also support Incest Survivors' Groups, which are self-help groups for adult women who have experienced sexual abuse by a trusted adult during their childhood.

The growth of rape crisis centres is directly attributable to the interest of the women's movement in the crime of rape, which itself symbolises the oppression of women by men in a patriarchal society. Rape crisis centres have a number of shared principles which underlie the response which they are able to give to women contacting them. Firstly, there is the belief that no woman is responsible for her own rape. Rape crisis centres accept without judgment whatever women want to tell and in so doing hope to begin to banish some of the guilt which a woman may feel. Secondly, rape crisis centres believe that all women share the threat of rape and male violence. This means that in giving support to a woman, a shared experience can reduce the potential for professional distancing. This is also reflected in the language used by collective members. For example, women who contact the centre are not referred to as 'victims' but as 'women who have been raped', and 'support' rather than 'counselling' is offered. Thirdly, any contact which a woman has with the rape crisis centre is totally confidential. If a woman is undecided about reporting the rape to the police, the rape crisis centre can explain police procedure and will be available to accompany her if she decides to report. Women are not persuaded either to report or to stay silent but are supported in whatever decision they make.

Rape crisis centres also campaign for the changing of public attitudes to rape. This is done by undertaking talks and using the media. They also engage in campaigns to draw attention to wider issues of violence against women. In Aberdeen, for example, the centre has successfully campaigned to prevent the establishment of sex shops in the city under the terms of the Civic Government (Scotland) Act 1982. It has also lodged objections to the city's Licencing Committee on issues relating to the portrayal of violence towards women in films and videos shown locally.

Many of the women who contact rape crisis centres call some time after the attack. Edinburgh RCC, in a sample of 50 consecutive calls, reported the following time lapse between the assault and contact with the Centre:

TABLE 5

Length of time between rape and contact with Edinburgh Rape Crisis Centre

Within a day	2%
Within a week	34%
Within a month	22%
Within 6 months	15%
Within a year	2%
Over a year	25%

Source: Edinburgh Rape Crisis Centre [4].

Other centres report a similar pattern.

In Aberdeen, the telephone line is open for just four hours each week. The rota is organised in advance, with two women available for each two-hour period. Working in pairs has the advantage of giving support to the woman taking the call, and sharing suggestions about what to say next. The Aberdeen collective does most of its training for the service 'on the job'. New members join the rota when they feel ready, and are paired with a more experienced member as far as possible. They choose when to start taking calls, although they often say that there is no better substitute than being 'dropped in at the deep end.' Record keeping is kept to a minimum, with all calls logged in a call book and a short coded record sheet completed. All of the work of the group is done, as far as possible, in pairs. This ensures that women support and learn from one another. Meeting with a caller is done in pairs, and the reasons for this are explained to her. During a meeting it is common for the woman to focus her attention on one person in the pair, and this enables the second woman to offer support afterwards. Having two women present is also helpful to reflect on the process and content of the meeting, and women can give supportive and honest feedback on how their partner handled the meeting. Collective working, with a strong emphasis on mutual support, has proved to be a successful model for rape crisis groups to operate on.

London Rape Crisis Centre have pointed out that a woman's first contact with a rape crisis centre is an important step in helping her to regain the control of her life which has been taken from her by the rape or sexual assault [22]. It is important to check out that the woman has contacted the centre because she wants to rather than because she has been pressurised into doing so. It is easy for well-meaning friends or professionals to alleviate

122

some of the woman's pain by making decisions for her. This only serves to reinforce her feelings of loss of control and it can create the feeling that she cannot look after herself. For this reason many rape crisis centres, including Aberdeen, are reluctant to take calls or referrals from third parties, most notably social workers or general practitioners. Experience has shown that if a woman feels that she has been pushed into contacting a rape crisis centre she is less likely to maintain contact and she may then feel more reluctant to renew contact at a later date. From time to time requests for information or support are made by family, friends or professionals. In these instances collective members give what support they can, and also try to encourage the caller to discuss contacting the rape crisis centre with the woman herself.

One of the most common feelings to be expressed by a woman, long after the assault, is that she should be 'over it by now'. It is often difficult for her to continue to talk about the rape and her reaction to it when people close to her expect her to forget about the experience and pick up the threads of her life again. Talking about the events of the assault is very painful, and many women never share details about the actual incident. Others want to talk about it in detail but cannot find the words to do so. In these instances women from the rape crisis centre can 'lead' the woman through the events, asking specific questions and helping to acknowledge the hurt and anger which she feels. It is important for the supportive person not to express inappropriately the anger which she herself may feel. Some women talk about the rape dispassionately, in the third person, as though it happened to someone else. This helps them to distance themselves from painful feelings. Initial fear can be turned to anger, and over time the burden of guilt can shift from the woman who has been violated to the perpetrator of the violent act.

In the process of giving support to a woman who has been raped, members of a rape crisis group can sometimes distance themselves from their own reactions to what has happened to the woman to whom they are offering support. The group tries to alert its members to the importance of acknowledging their own feelings of anger, hurt and powerlessness, and to recognise that emotional distancing may be one way of denying one's own vulnerability. Alpert and Schechter [27] have pointed out that:

> 'a lack of insight into one's own emotional reactions may also lead to premature burnout with resultant feelings of personal failure, depression and anger.'

Rape crisis members are encouraged to examine their feelings about violence and their personal reaction to it. Alpert and Schechter [27] advocate:

'sensitising exercises, focussing on the worker's own victimisation and mourning experiences. . . . to enable them to understand their own vulnerabilities and reactions to victimisation . . . . no-one is free from fears.'

Many feelings may be common to both the abused woman and the rape crisis centre member – for example, feelings of personal helplessness may lead both women to feel overwhelmed and frightened. It often helps to acknowledge that any woman could experience sexual violence and that the women who are supported by rape crisis centres are in many ways no different from members of the collective.

Alpert and Schechter [27] have produced a useful set of responses and actions for giving support to women who have been raped in which they have identified common feelings, anxieties and frustrations. They suggest, for example, that both women may feel intense anger, but that it is inappropriate for the supportive woman to ventilate her anger, as this only reinforces the raped woman's guilt and sense of responsibility for what has happened.

INCEST SURVIVORS' GROUPS

Many of the calls which are received by rape crisis centres are from women who have been sexually abused in their childhood by a trusted adult. When the Aberdeen rape crisis centre opened in 1982 this was not an area to which the group had given much thought. At that time sexual abuse of children was rarely discussed openly and few of the helping agencies locally could offer an adequate support service for adults who had suffered such abuse. Since then, however, social work departments and the health service have become much more aware of the issue; more training and resources are diverted towards work with children who are living in an abusive situation, but there have been fewer developments in support for adult women.

Since Aberdeen rape crisis centre opened, almost half of all the calls received have been from incest survivors. Often the calls are from women who are 'telling the secret' for the first time and the support offered to them by the group is on an individual basis or as members of an Incest Survivors' Group, which was established in 1985. The group members identify themselves as survivors, because they have broken the silence surrounding their abuse, and because they no longer see themselves as 'victims'. More than 20 women have attended the group which currently meets on a three week cycle.

Two members of the rape crisis group, neither of whom have experienced sexual abuse, attend the meetings, and they share responsibility for facilitating the group discussion. Sometimes a theme or issue has been identified during one meeting, and plans are made to follow it up at a subsequent meeting. The rape crisis members usually take the responsibility for this. The group also allows time for members to share their current anxieties and feelings and an enormous amount of support is gained from group membership. The group sometimes uses exercises from a book of self help therapy [28] as a means of getting in touch with feelings or situations which are painful.

The mechanism for joining the Incest Survivors' Group is that women contact the rape crisis centre in the first instance, and an arrangement is made for a meeting with one of the survivors and a rape crisis member. Information is shared about the group, and the potential new member usually arranges to meet with her contacts again prior to attending her first group meeting. This gives her the choice of opting out if she chooses to do so or, if she decides to join the group, she is able to be introduced to this new experience by a familiar person. The survivors' group has a small core of women who attend on a regular basis; other women have attended on one or two occasions and a number have stopped attending and return to the group when they feel the need to do so. Group members often comment on the 'common language' which exists between them, and their diverse life experiences have many common threads which enable them to draw support from one another.

RAPE CRISIS CENTRES AND THE CRIMINAL JUSTICE SYSTEM

Rape crisis centres are more firmly established in the United States, where they receive substantial federal government support for staff and research funds. Between 1973 and 1981 the United States government gave grants to an estimated total of 125 million dollars for the study of rape and sexual assault [9]. By 1971 Amir was able to note that rape crisis centres had been established in 65 per cent of all communities and 95 per cent of large cities in America. Centres have had an uneasy relationship with police and other branches of the criminal justice system, as they lobby fiercely for women's rights to better treatment in the hands of the police and criminal justice system. In the United States the relationships have markedly improved, as cooperation has been achieved on the drawing up of policy and procedural guidelines. Blair [9] conducted a survey of American and British rape crisis centres and their relationship with their local police force. He asked the police to rate the level of cooperation with local centres.

TABLE 6

Relationship between selected rape crisis centres and their local police force

	Great Britain %	United States %
Very cooperative	26	65
Somewhat cooperative	57	32
Not cooperative	26	3

Source: Blair, I. [9].

The police view is that there are two main barriers to good communication with rape crisis centres. Firstly the lack of 'trained' paid staff which limits the availability of the service, and secondly, a lack of mainstream funding. In Britain the emergence of Victim Support Schemes, which have the backing of most police authorities, has led in some instances to the police referring women to these schemes rather than to rape crisis centres.

At the same time, there are a number of interesting developments within police forces themselves which are indicative of a shift in attitudes and a more supportive response to women who have been raped. Some of these developments, from both sides of the Atlantic, are described below.

A More Supportive Response by the Police?

The shift in attitudes and practice by the police has been most marked in the United States and has been characterised by five features. Firstly, medical offence investigations, including rape, are restricted to specialist teams of officers. Secondly, these teams undergo intensive training and selection for the team is on the basis of personal qualities. Thirdly, the teams, where they exist, are a prestigious feature of the forces in which they operate. Fourthly, they have a good relationship with the local prosecutor, and fifthly, they are committed to a high degree of collaboration with external resources for the support and aftercare of women who have been raped or sexually assaulted.

In San Fransisco, for example, where the Police Department employs more than 2,500 officers to serve a population of 850,000], there is a Sex Crimes Detail, comprising nine detectives and a lieutenant [9]. The Sex Crimes Detail is a prestigious unit, and serving officers are drawn from other detective units. The District Attorney's Office also has a staff of four who deal exclusively with crimes involving sex and there is a 24-hour service within the Public Health Department which provides facilities for forensic examinations. A team of trained counsellors who maintain contact with the raped woman after she has been to the unit is also available. Women are not interviewed by the police until the Sexual Trauma Service has given them the support they require. This means that when women are eventually interviewed by the police they are beginning to regain some control over their life situations. It is also evident that the high repute afforded to the Rape Trauma Service has had a beneficial effect on police reputation.

In Britain, changes in police investigation practice and in the treatment of women who allege rape have been less marked. Since 1980, however, there has been a shift in attitudes. The Heilbron Report [29] did not contain recommendations on police procedure but, following some well publicised negative judicial statements in rape trials, the issue of rape was projected into the public arena. Another event which helped to encourage public debate was the 'Glasgow Rape Case' when a charge of rape was dropped because the chief witness was considered unable to give evidence due to her mental state after a particularly brutal attack [30]. The handling of the case forced the resignation of the Solicitor General for Scotland, and the woman eventually brought a successful private prosecution against her rapists.

In 1983 the Scottish Office published a report by two of its own researchers which provided a critical account of police investigating procedures in cases of sexual assault [10]. The researchers found that for women reporting a rape, police interviewing practices were experienced as the most stressful feature of the whole investigation. The report made a number of important observations and recommended increased specialisation in the area of sexual assault, more police training and the undertaking of medical examinations in a hospital or surgery setting, rather than in the police station. The report also stressed the importance of support for the complainer and advocated closer collaboration with rape crisis centres.

> 'Many police officers. . . . are only vaguely aware of the existence of these groups. Contacts . . . . would be better if specialist units existed and if some meetings could take place to discuss how follow-up assistance and advice could best be provided' [10].

In 1985, taking account of the findings of the report, the Scottish Home and Health Department issued a circular for Chief Constables on the investigation of complaints of sexual assault. The circular advocated a more humane treatment of the complainers, a review of police questioning procedures and medical examinations and a recognition of the psychological effects of rape and sexual assault [31]. The final circular incorporated many of the comments on the original draft, which were made by rape crisis centres and other organisations concerned with violence towards women. It is perhaps too early to say if lasting changes have occurred within Scottish police forces, but there have been developments elsewhere in the country.

The Metropolitan Police, for example, has increased its female forensic medical staff from 12 women in 1983 to 24 in 1986, out of a total of 99. Thelma Wagstaff, one of only two female Commanders in the Metropolitan Police and Chair of their Working Party on Rape, has helped to establish nine special examination suites across London. Fifteen detectives and 12 women police officers are permanently assigned to rape cases [32].

In Manchester, the Police and Health authority are collaborating in the establishment of a Sexual Assault Referral Centre, to which contact can be made after a rape without the police being informed. The centre will be staffed by female nurses and counsellors and there will be no pressure to report the assault to the police [33].

Behind both of these initiatives lies the hope that by making a high quality and sensitive service available to women, they will be encouraged to report sexual assaults. Commander Wagstaff has noted:

> 'Unless women do report, there is no way the police or the public actually know the extent of the problem. . . . We are trying to make it less embarrassing for a woman to report a rape to the police. We are trying to be more caring' [34].

CONCLUDING COMMENT

Griffin [34] has asserted that rape is consistent with society's view of women. She suggests that rape becomes justified in a society where women are oppressed by men. It could therefore be argued that if our society is to tackle squarely the issues raised by men's continued violence towards women, it must also examine the nature of its patriarchal institutions. It has taken the efforts of women themselves to challenge these institutions and to establish their own support systems for women who have been sexually assaulted by men. It is now surely the time for the rest of society to respond with a change in attitudes and ultimately in the relationship between men and women.

References

1. Dukes, R.L. & Mattley, C.L. 'Predicting Rape Victim Reportage' *Sociology and Social Research*. 62, 1, 1977.

2. Hough, M. & Mayhew, P. *The British Crime Survey*. Home Office Research Study No.76, HMSO, London, 1983.

3. London Rape Crisis Centre Rape Counselling and Research Project. *Rape, Police and Forensic Practice*. Evidence submitted to the Royal Commission on Criminal Procedure, London, 1978.

4. Edinburgh Rape Crisis Centre. *First Report*. Edinburgh, 1981.

5. Aberdeen Rape Crisis Centre. Unpublished Centre Statistics. Aberdeen, 1986.

6. Birmingham Rape Crisis Centre. Report, 1980. Birmingham, 1981.

7. Hanmer, J. & Saunders, S. *Well-founded Fear: A Community Study of Violence to Women*. Hutchinson, London, 1984.

8. Hall, R. *Ask Any Woman. A London Inquiry into Rape and Sexual Assault. Report of the Women's Safety Survey conducted by Women Against Rape*. Falling Wall Press, Bristol, 1985.

9. Blair, I. *Investigating Rape: A New Approach for Police*. Croom Helm, Dover, 1985.

10. Chambers, G. & Millar, A. *Investigating Sexual Assault*. Scottish Office Central Research Unit, Edinburgh. HMSO, 1983.

11. Katz, S. & Mazur, M. *Understanding the Rape Victim*. John Wiley & Sons, New York, 1979.

12. Amir, M. *Patterns in Forcible Rape*. University of Chicago Press, Chicago, 1971.

13. Wright, R. 'The English Rapist' *New Society*. 17th July, 1980.

14. Troner, B. *The Facts of Rape*. Arrow Books, London, 1977.

15. Taylor, A., quoted in Griffin, S. 'Rape: The All-American Crime' *Ramparts*. 10, 9, 1971.

16. Home Office. *Criminal Statistics, England and Wales, 1980*. Cmnd. 8376, HMSO, London, 1982.

17. Quoted in Patullo, P. *Judging Women*. National Council for Civil Liberties, London, 1983.

18. Chappell, D. & Singer, S. 'Rape in New York City'. In Chappell, D., Geis, G. & Geis, R. *Forcible Rape: The Crime, the Victim and the Offender*. Columbia University Press, 1977.

19. Brownmillar, S. *Against Our Will: Men, Women and Rape*. Penguin, Harmondsworth, 1973.

20. Groth, N. *Men Who Rape*. Plenum, London, 1978.

21. Burgess, A. & Holstromn, L. 'Rape Trauma Syndrome' *American Journal of Psychiatry.* 121, 9, 1974.

22. London Rape Crisis Centre. *Sexual Violence: The Reality for Women.* The Women's Press Handbook Series, London, 1984.

23. Lindemann, E. 'Symptomatology and Management of Grief' *American Journal of Psychology.* 101, 1944.

24. Basuk, E. 'Crisis Theory Perspective on Rape'. In McCombe, S.L. (Ed.) *Rape Crisis Intervention Handbook.* Plenum Press, New York, 1980.

25. Weis, K. & Borgess, E.V. 'Victimology and Rape: The Case of the Legitimate Victim'. In Schultz, L. (Ed.) *Rape Victimology.* Charles C. Thomas, Illinois, 1975.

26. Rowland, J. *Rape: The Ultimate Violation.* Pluto Press, London, 1986.

27. Alpert, M. & Schechter, S. 'Sensitising Workers to the Needs of Victims: Common Worker and Victim Responses' *Victimology*, 4, 4, 1979.

28. Ernst, S. & Goodison, L. *In Our Own Hands: A Book of Self-Help Therapy.* The Women's Press, London, 1981.

29. Home Office. *Report of the Advisory Group on the Law of Rape* (Heilbron Report). Cmnd 6352, HMSO, London, 1975.

30. Harper, R. & McWhinnie, A. *The Glasgow Rape Case.* Hutchinson, London, 1983.

31. Scottish Home and Health Department. 'Investigation of Complaints of Sexual Assault.' Circular 7/1985, Edinburgh.

32. Evans, P. 'Police Soften Attitudes to Victims' *The Times.* 25th January, 1985.

33. Personal correspondence with Manchester Police, July, 1986.

34. Ballantyne, A. 'Softly, Softly Approach to Rape Victims' *Guardian*, 13 August, 1986.

Working with Sex Offenders

Derek Perkins*

INTRODUCTION

Sex offending is a subject which has the potential to arouse a wide range of emotions – disgust, anger, sympathy in relation to victim or offender, anxiety about our own sexual attitudes and behaviour, and general public concern that effective action should be taken to combat the problem.

Theoretically, sex offending can be reviewed in a number of ways. Systems of analysis range from the socio-cultural context of sex offending to the idiosyncratic patterns of sexual arousal displayed by individual offenders. Each level of analysis is relevant to a full understanding of the other levels.

The various models of sex offending use different methods of analysis. Socio-cultural theories are usually supported by data from criminal statistics and community surveys. Psychological theories tend to rely most heavily on self-report and psychometric data, and on the observation of patterns of interpersonal behaviour. At the level of sexual interests and arousal, psychophysiological assessment is the procedure most commonly reported.

PRESENTING FOR TREATMENT

Sex offenders can present for medical or psychological treatment in a number of ways. Typically, they do so only after action has been taken along the continuum of detection-apprehension-prosecution, which brings them into contact with one or more of those professionals who will then be required to comment upon their offending behaviour and the possibility of it being amenable to treatment.

The professionals most likely to assess and comment upon sex offending

*The views expressed are those of the author and are not necessarily those of the DHSS.

behaviour and its treatability prior to cases coming to court are clinical psychologists, forensic psychiatrists, social workers and probation officers. Offenders in prison, either on remand or subsequent to conviction, if assessed at all, will tend to be seen by prison psychologists, medical officers or probation officers. Each professional will approach this task from a somewhat different standpoint.

The social enquiry reports prepared by probation officers or social workers usually deal in detail with the offender's current circumstances in the natural environment. Forensic psychiatrists are particularly well equipped to detect, and make recommendations in relation to matters of psychiatric disability and fitness to plead. Clinical psychologists, on the other hand, tend to deal in depth with the personality and environmental precipitants of the sex offending behaviour which has brought the offender to his present position before the court or into prison.

TREATABILITY

Treatability, at its simplest, concerns the feasibility of modifying particular elements of behaviour, in particular contexts, by particular methods and with particular resources.

The behaviour in question may range from indecent exposure, likely to be dealt with by non-custodial means, to violent rape or sexually motivated aggression, which are likely to result in incarceration for the offender.

The context of sex offending can be described by both the inter-personal features of the offence situation (e.g. rape carried out on a stranger by a delinquent sub-group) as well as its physical and socio-economic features (e.g. inner city area with high unemployment).

The methods employed to effect behaviour modification might range from those focussed on the functioning of individual offenders (psycho-surgery, behaviour therapy, medication, directive advice and so on) to those applying to many individuals across a particular situation (censorship, more police on the beat, improved recreational facilities and so on). With those behaviour change methods focussed on individuals, interventions tend to be conceptualised as 'therapy' or 'punishment'. Where interventions are applied to many individuals across a situation, this tends to be conceptualised as 'social or political policy'.

Both the 'individualised' and 'socio-political' interventions may or may not achieve their desired objectives. In terms of the 'socio-political' approach,

Tutt [1], for example, has commented on the sometimes paradoxical effects of changes in the law or social policy. For the 'individualised' approach to treatment, the outcomes of treatment efficacy research vary from study to study depending on client groups, treatments and evaluation methods used.

At the level of individualised treatments, to which the notion of treatability is most commonly related, questions of the sort, 'is offender X treatable?' will require consideration at all four of the levels just considered. If resources are adequate, then it may be that a particular offender (e.g. a socially inadequate and sexually deviant aggressive offender) will be responsive to a combination of treatment methods (e.g. social skills training, re-direction of deviant sexual interests and group therapy discussions of sexual attitudes) within the context of, for example, a low security prison, such that his self-esteem and social/sexual achievements may be developed to a degree which is incompatible with further offending.

Perkins [2] has argued that individualised treatments are most appropriately pursued where the sex offending behaviour in question is most readily understood or predicted by reference to the characteristics of the individual offender. In such cases, offending behaviour is likely to have been exhibited frequently, in many situations and over a long period of time. It is in such cases as these that the offender is most likely to see 'something wrong' with himself and hence be more amenable to the notion of individualised treatment.

Treatability is likely to be greatest where there is political and public support for the philosophy behind the treatment, where appropriate resources are available, where the offender has engaged in repeated and specific socially unacceptable behaviour which has adverse consequences for him and where, perhaps as a result of this, he sees something wrong with his behaviour which might be amenable to individualised treatment.

TREATMENT

Sex offender treatment, that aims to reduce the possibility of future sex offending from the level it would have maintained without treatment, involves an understanding of three sorts of information. First, the results of research into the nature of sex offending, from which the various levels on which the problem occurs can be identified:

(a) Social climate – the public perceptions of men, women and children, their rights and the ways in which they are depicted in the media.

(b) Interpersonal relationship – offenders with their victims, and the relationships of offenders and victims with their relatives, friends and acquaintances.

(c) Attitudes and feelings – of the offender about himself, about his victim and about the nature of his offending.

(d) Sexual interests and arousal patterns – of offenders in relation to the acts and subjects of their offending, and in relation to the non-deviant sexual interests they would hope to develop as alternatives to offending.

(e) The offending environment – public and police responses at the scenes of offences, probabilities of detection and conviction, and opportunities for offending which either occur naturally or are actively created by the offender.

Secondly, there are the results of studies concerning particular methods of treatment which have been used with sex offenders – social skills training, reconditioning of sexual interests, and so on.

Thirdly, in order to embark upon a treatment, an analysis is required of the individual offender's history (educational, social and sexual) and the particular features of his offence behaviour (the acts he has committed, and their antecedents and consequences).

The three types of data which have been identified, namely the nature of particular classes of sex offending, the outcomes of particular treatment methods and the details of particular offenders' histories and patterns of offending, represent overlapping systems of knowledge, each of which is important in establishing appropriate systems of treatment.

At the widest, sociological level of analysis, the design of our environment, the nature of our justice system and the relative provisions of various educative, treatment and counselling services are all areas of potential intervention in dealing with the issue of sex offending. Changes in any of these systems can, in a sense, be a 'treatment response' by society to the problem of sexual crime.

At the opposite end of the spectrum are the interventions directed at modifying the behaviour of individual offenders. The fact that sexual recidivism exists, some individuals persisting in seriously assaultive behaviour over many years, means that individual treatment programmes will continue to be an important component of policy concerned with the issue of sexual crime.

Approaches to the individual treatment of sex offenders can be classified in terms of the theoretical models from which they emanate – psychoanalytic or behavioural, for example – or in terms of their therapeutic aims – reducing deviant sexual interest, enhancing non-deviant interest, improving social skills, and so on.

In examining the operational details of different theoretical approaches, it is evident that there is considerable overlap in the procedures employed. Abel and Blanchard's [3] review of the role of fantasy in the treatment of sexual deviation highlights some striking parallels between psychodynamic and behavioural approaches.

Within a broadly behavioural framework, the treatment of individual offenders will follow from two considerations. First, the definitions of problems and goals, in which both the offender and the therapist are involved, will specify as clearly as possible the behaviours, attitudes, interests etc. to be eliminated and those to be developed. Secondly, functional relationships will be sought between the offender's behaviour (both desirable and undesirable) and factors within his environment.

The process of behavioural analysis which works to this end seeks to identify those assets and deficits within the individual's behavioural repertoire and factors within his environment which maintain deviant behaviour and those factors which will assist in the development of alternative, desirable behaviours. It is on the manipulation of these personality and environmental factors, that treatment will concentrate.

PRE-CONDITIONS FOR OFFENDING

Finkelhor [4] has proposed a sequential system of four pre-conditions which need to be met before sexual abuse of children can occur. Although developed in connection specifically with offences against children, Finkelhor's model probably has wider applicability.

In reviewing factors relating to the commission of sexual offences against children, Finkelhor proposed that they can be grouped under four headings, each representing a pre-condition for offending to occur, each pre-condition representing a characteristic of the offender, of the victim or of the offence situation which will turn a potential offender into an actual offender.

These four pre-conditions can be summarised as:

(a) A potential offender needs to have some motivation to abuse a child sexually.

(b) A potential offender has to overcome internal inhibitions against acting on that motivation.

(c) A potential offender has to overcome external impediments to committing sexual offending.

(d) A potential offender, or some other factor has to undermine or overcome a child's possible resistance to the sexual offence.

From each of these stages, particular forms of intervention might be proposed. The first two stages clearly imply individual treatment directed to the offender, but the second two stages might equally involve attention being focussed on features of environments in which sexual offending might occur and to the education and training of potential victims.

Such education and training is well established in the USA, and is now being developed in the United Kingdom. At the time of writing, 75 per cent of ten year old school children have seen the Home Office film, 'Say No to a Stranger', which has also been shown on television.

Again developed from work in the USA, Clinical Psychologist Michelle Elliott's 'Child Assault Prevention Programme' is now being used in British schools [5]. Through various exercises, including role-playing, children are taught how to get the better of would-be molesters. Similar initiatives are being developed by other agencies, including the Rape Crisis Centres [6].

Some notes of caution have been sounded in connection with this work [7], Tucker arguing that some children may be encouraged to be unduly suspicious of adults, uncooperative with, or make false allegations against them, and indeed that some adults may become so sensitised to a climate of child sexual abuse that they suppress their own non-harmful, affectionate responses to children. The general view, however, is that the present developments are more than justified given the extent of sexual abuse and that the balance is strongly in favour of alerting children and responsible adults to the dangers of sexual offending and ways of counteracting it.

Extrapolating from Finkelhor's model of child sexual abuse to sexual offending generally, it is now well established that under-reporting occurs in all classes of sexual offence. A general population survey carried out in the USA [8] found that 19 per cent of women students and 9 per cent of men students reported some sexual experience with an adult in their childhood. Also in 1980, the British Association for the Study and Prevention of Child Abuse published a report [9] estimating that one in eight females and one in ten males suffers sexual abuse during their childhood.

Even conservative estimates of under-reporting in cases of rape, suggest that about 50 per cent of rapes are not reported to the police. A survey of indecent exposure experienced by a sample of women in England [10] found that 44 per cent had witnessed acts of indecent exposure, making the rate of under-reporting for this offence enormous. In cases of incest and the sexual abuse of children within families, the massive scale of the phenomenon is only now becoming known.

FAMILY AND NON-FAMILY SEXUAL OFFENDING

A major parameter in considering sex offender treatment is the extent to which offending is perpetrated against those known to the perpetrator, most notably within the family situation, as opposed to being perpetrated against strangers. This is no simple dichotomy, however, but rather a continuum embracing assaults by casual acquaintances, friends of the family, relatives not living within the home, and so on.

Nevertheless, it is perhaps relevant in considering treatment issues to examine some of the particular features applying first to sexual offending within families and, secondly, to sexual offending against strangers or casual acquaintances. The case material used to illustrate this discussion will be drawn from the psychological treatment programme for sex offenders at Birmingham Prison and All Saints Hospital outpatient clinic which is reported in detail elsewhere [2,11,12].

SEXUAL ABUSE WITHIN FAMILIES

Within family settings, most sexual abuse is perpetrated against girls by their fathers or step-fathers [13]. There will be many pressures operating against the victims of sexual abuse reporting these offences to someone in authority. Fear of violence from the father, fear of the family being split up, fear of losing the father's affection or other tangible rewards, and guilt experienced by the child about her (or his) own behaviour are some of the more obvious of these pressures.

A typical pattern in the sexual abuse of daughters by their fathers or step-fathers is that offending begins at a relatively early age, usually when the girl is aged about 10, and continues for between several months and several years. Often, escalating demands are made on the child. The child not reporting this offending can become the basis of the father's rationalisation that the daughter was a willing partner to what took place. There are many other rationalisations which are said to be used by incestuous fathers in order to excuse their behaviour. Amongst these are:

(a) No longer being sexually aroused by their wives.
(b) Their wives not being interested in sex.
(c) Incest being morally preferable to adultery.
(d) Adultery being likely to break up the home.
(e) That the men have a greater need for sex than other men.
(f) That incest is a valuable introduction to sex for the children.

In discussing the question of rationalisations, we enter a difficult area where questions of moral responsibility and objective analysis of causation can become easily confused. To take a quite different example, to say that an unlocked car or an unlockable car is a factor in the level of 'take and drive away' offences is perhaps self-evident. However, to say that a woman walking alone at night dressed in a particular way is a factor in a rape offence is likely to be controversial.

In the assessment and treatment of some rapists, it might be that the presence of the woman in the way described could be a factor in the man having committed the offence. This does not, however, remove responsibility for the offence from that man, even though some judges have made statements of this kind.

Police advice to women in the form of brochures suggesting how the probability of rape might be reduced if women avoided risky situations by curtailing their movements have quite understandably provoked adverse reactions from women's groups. Although objectively the advice is correct, the objection to it stems from its assumption that it is women rather than men who should change their patterns of behaviour, and restrict their freedom, in order to reduce the probability of offending.

When we turn to incest and other forms of child sexual abuse within the family, there is a similar paradox. Legally and morally, the male offender is required, quite rightly, to accept responsibility for his behaviour. However, in terms of a behavioural analysis of his offending, attempts will be made to link his offence behaviour to its antecedents and consequences in ways which might open up possibilities for treatment. Although these explanations will be framed within the 'objective' mode with a view to minimising future offending, they will often be construed within the 'moral' code as providing the man with rationalisations for his offending, which will be seen to detract from his accepting responsibility for his actions.

It might well be that, for various reasons, the man is no longer sexually aroused by his wife; it may be, for various reasons, that the wife is no longer interested in sexual activity with her husband; it may be, in terms of various parameters, that the man does indeed have a greater sexual drive than other men. These facts are not to deny his responsibility for his offending, but they may still be facts which need to be addressed if repetitions of offending are not to occur.

Questions of punishment and treatment are central to the way in which offenders perpetrating sexual abuse within the family are dealt with by the courts. The court will need to consider the public's condemnation of the offence, and the corresponding level at which the offender should be pubished. It will need to consider the risks of further offending if the man is not imprisoned, and it will need to consider the possibilities of long term rehabilitation.

There is a further consideration, and one which is difficult to deal with satisfactorily in this country, and that is the competing needs of victims – to effect reconciliation with perpetrators as opposed to seeing perpetrators punished for their offending. In Great Britain, where offences of sexual abuse against children come to light, prosecutions have often followed regardless of the additional harm that this may inflict upon the victims of those offences.

By contrast, in Israel there is a system in which the child victims of sexual abuse are first interviewed by so-called youth interrogators. These individuals are trained social workers, psychologists or psychiatrists and need to give their permission before the police are allowed to take legal action against the perpetrator. In a study of over a thousand child victims, permission for the child to testify in court was given in only 14 per cent of cases where the child was over ten years of age and in only eight per cent of cases where the child was under ten years of age [14].

Although this evidence is indirect as far as Great Britain is concerned, the implications for current practice would be that between 80 and 90 per cent of children who presently testify in court proceedings in relation to sexual victimisation may well be more adversely affected by the process than would have been the case had matters been dealt with by non-legal means.

In Holland, there is a system for dealing with child sexual abuse focused on the so-called confidential doctor, who will undertake therapy with families where child sexual abuse has come to light. The system has sometimes been referred to as one of 'benign blackmail', in that police involvement can be initiated by the confidential doctor should the male perpetrator fail to co-operate in treatment. Under these circumstances, not surprisingly, most perpetrators do take part in treatment, often with satisfactory outcome.

Giaretto [15], in the USA, reported a similar treatment programme for the families of father-daughter incest. Between 1971 and 1978, over six hundred families were seen, and about 90 per cent of the children previously offended against were returned to their families. Reconviction rates at the time of Giaretto's report were less than one per cent.

Similar initiatives have been developed in Great Britain, notably at the great Ormond Street Hospital for Children. A multi-disciplinary working party report [16], reviewing the nature of child sexual abuse within the family, recommended that the protection and welfare of the child concerned should be the primary concern of all those dealing with child sexual abuse cases.

It was further recommended that investigation of suspected cases of child sexual abuse within families should take both legal and therapeutic factors into account, and that multi-disciplinary collaboration, involving police, social services departments, the NSPCC and other treatment agencies, should be established, and that multi-disciplinary teams should be involved in the management and treatment of child sexual abuse cases.

SEXUAL ABUSE OUTSIDE THE FAMILY

While it can be the case that the most helpful thing for victims of sexual abuse within the family will be for the professionals concerned to help the family towards reconciliation while ensuring that no further sexual offending occurs, and this might mean the perpetrator remaining out of prison, there will be no such rationale for keeping sexual offenders against strangers out of prison.

Some sexual offenders against strangers may be suitable for treatment in the community, but the benefit of this will be weighed carefully by the courts against the risks of further offending should the offender remain at liberty and the degree of moral outrage generated by the offence. Although all three of these sentencing principles can sometimes be accommodated simultaneously by imposing an appropriately retributive sentence of imprisonment with an expectation that the offender might receive treatment both while in prison and after his release, it is the case that some perpetrators who might be inclined to accept treatment if this were provided in the context of a non-custodial disposal (perhaps linked to a probation order) will not be so enthusiastic to embark upon treatment after a period of imprisonment when there are no further legal restrictions which can be brought into play.

Within the prison or Special Hospital setting, certain features of an offender's offence behaviour may be amenable to analysis and treatment. The presence or absence of deviant sexual interest, for example, can be assessed within an institution by means of self-report and psychophysiological data. Deficient social skills can similarly be assessed to some degree within an institution by means of self-report, roleplays and observations of interpersonal behaviour.

The success of such institutionally-based treatments can be short-lived, however, problems arising when the offender comes to be released back into the community. First, there is the question of 'generalisation'; that is whether the changes in the offender's behaviour which have been established within the institution will carry over into the real world. Often they will not since the institutional environment is usually quite different, physically and socially, from the natural environment. Secondly, since there is considerable control over the offender's behaviour within the institution, not least in connection with decisions about when he is to be released, he may well be inclined to co-operate with treatment endeavours within the institution which he may well then abandon upon his release.

Turning to the specific treatment techniques which might be employed with incarcerated sex offenders or sex offenders in the community, a broad distinction can be drawn between problems of deviant sexual interest and problems of socio-sexual behaviour. Whilst these techniques have been reported primarily in the treatment of sexual offenders outside the family setting, there will be elements from these procedures which could equally well be applied to working with perpetrators of sexual abuse within the family.

Where offenders are sexually aroused by deviant acts (for example, sadism) or by other than consenting adult partners (for example, children), these deviant interests can be assessed by a combination of self-report, behavioural and psychophysiological assessment. Typically, an offender might be asked to indicate on self-report protocols, his sexual interest in various visual material or audiotaped descriptions of sexual activity. His penile erection responses to this material can be assessed by means of a penile plethysmograph [17,18,19,20]. His sexual behaviour and fantasies can also be monitored before, during and after treatment. In combination, this information can contribute to an understanding of his pattern of sexual interest at the outset of treatment and subsequently.

Treatment of deviant sexual interest involves both decreasing deviant sexual interest and enhancing non-deviant sexual interest. One approach to the decrease of deviant sexual interest is aversion therapy, in which deviant material is systematically paired with unpleasant stimulation, for example, mild electric shocks [21], unpleasant imagery [22], or unpleasant social consequences such as being shamed by observers [23].

The enhancement of non-deviant sexual interest has been reported as a by-product of some of the aversive procedures [24], as well as by the more direct procedures of masturbatory conditioning, where the offender systematically replaces deviant masturbation fantasies with those of a non-deviant kind [25].

The behaviour procedure of systematic desensitisation has also been used to increase non-deviant sexual interest through a process of gradually exposing offenders to the anxiety-provoking aspects of non-deviant sexual activity which may have previously deterred them from engaging in such activity [11].

In addition to deviant sexual interests which sex offenders may or may not exhibit, they almost inevitably experience problems of social and sexual relationships. Many offenders are either anxious in, or do not possess the skills necessary to function adequately within adult social or sexual situations. Some sexual offenders against children may act in this way largely as a result of social inadequacies or anxieties with adults.

Assessment methods for the behavioural aspects of sex offenders' interpersonal problems are less well developed than those dealing with sexual interests, largely because such procedures are more difficult to set up than laboratory-based procedures for the assessment of sexual interests. Nevertheless, interview data provided by offenders and those who know them have usefully been supplemented by data from analogues of social activities, such as roleplayed conversations with female 'stooges', dealing with issues such as social perception, conversational skills or temper-control.

Perhaps the most widely reported procedure for dealing with problems of socio-sexual behaviour of sex offenders is social skills training [26]. Rehearsal and feedback of role-played interactions relevant to the offender's circumstances are the central features of the procedure, often being supplemented by coaching and modelling by the therapist, other social skills trainees or audio/videotape material.

Cognitive behaviour modification [27] is becoming increasingly recognised as a therapeutic procedure of value in the treatment of sexual offending. The approach involves intervening directly at the level of the offender's thoughts, for example, by eliciting the typical trains of thought which accompany the sex offender's build-ups to, and perpetration of sexual offences.

Empathic therapeutic relationships [25] are recognised to be a common element in many treatment programmes for sex offenders, although there is little consistency in the way such aspects of treatment are reported. Empathic therapeutic relationships can be the starting point for dealing with issues of eliciting sensitive information from offenders and in dealing with the issue of denial.

These various, above-mentioned aspects of treatment often overlap. Crawford [28] has emphasised the importance of 'broad-based' approaches to treatment with sex offenders. He has suggested that treatment should build up in a logical sequence the skills and knowledge which the offender will need in order to achieve success in conventional social settings, for example learning appropriate social skills before moving on to mastering appropriate sexual skills. Perkins [10], on the other hand, noting that each offender presents a unique blend of problems and assets, argues that there can often be a central 'core' of problems which, once dealt with, can 'unblock' other barriers to normal functioning, e.g. increased self-esteem leading naturally on to an increased preparedness to enter into social situations, leading to increased positive feedback on social functioning, leading to an increased willingness to mix socially with members of the opposite sex, leading to satisfactory heterosexual relationships.

For the treatment of sex offenders in prison and in Special Hospital to be followed through to its logical conclusion, a continuation of the process into the post-release period is essential. This is partly so as to consolidate within the offender's natural environment any changes brought about within the institutional setting, and partly because some problems can only be tackled in the natural environment, for example interpersonal functioning within the family situation or patterns of alcohol/drug use and abuse.

CASE STUDIES:

John

John was 32 years of age when first referred for possible treatment while on remand in Birmingham Prison. His level of intelligence was formerly assessed as being within the borderline mentally impaired range. He lived at home with his parents and brother and worked part-time in a public house. Over the year or so prior to his conviction for sexual assaults on a number of girls, he had been involved in numerous sexual acts with girls aged between approximately seven to ten years, both around the pub where he worked and in the vicinity of his home.

From interview and psychophysiological assessment, his sexual interest was primarily directed towards young girls. He had, in effect, been punished by his parents for embryonic sexual relationships he had begun to establish with girls of his own age when he was in his teens. In contrast, there had been no punishment for his sexual involvements with young girls, which had been carried out secretly. The difficulties he had experienced in his attempts at sexual relationships with girls of his own age had, it seemed, left him with feelings of anxiety surrounding adult heterosexual relationships, including what amounted to almost phobic reactions to certain adult female characteristics, notably pubic hair.

In addition to the social difficulties he experienced with women, and the correspondingly more comfortable feelings he enjoyed with young girls, together with his high sexual interest in young girls and the low sexual interest, and almost revulsion, he experienced in contemplating adult heterosexual relationships, he also exhibited a mode of thinking which appeared to reinforce his deviant activities. Specifically, he expressed on a number of occasions, during his imprisonment, the idea that his offending against young girls was not particularly wrong, that it would be of no harm to the children concerned and that, in any case, in other countries this kind of activity was not illegal. These attitudes appeared to gain in momentum as he approached his point of release from prison.

Treatment with John lasted over two years, both in prison and in the community, and passed through a number of phases involving at different times aversion therapy directed towards his deviant sexual interest in young girls, participation in social skills training directed toward equipping him with the skills and confidence necessary to relate better to people of his own age, systematic desensitisation designed to eliminate the anxiety and revulsion he felt towards adult females and, finally surrogate therapy (organised through another agency) in which he achieved for the first time satisfactory sexual intercourse with an adult female partner.

When followed up four years later, John had not re-offended. He was one of a number of offenders who fell within the 'treatment successful' category of research on the outcome of a broad based behavioural programme for sex offenders reported elsewhere.

David

David's sexual offending was of a different kind, being carried out entirely within the family. He and his wife had been married for a number of years and had three children – two girls and a younger boy. David and his wife were very different in personality. She presented as verbal, sociable and able to express her feelings. He, because of childhood experiences in which he had been condemned and ridiculed, was much less sociable, found it difficult to express his feelings, tended towards self pity and was inclined to opt out of interpersonal difficulties rather than face them.

A pattern had developed within this family wherein the wife turned increasingly for her emotional, but not her sexual satisfaction to other people, and David, although experiencing anger and anxiety about various aspects of their relationship, failed to introduce these feelings into the discussions about their marriage which his wife periodically stimulated.

As time went by, David became unemployed and took on increasing child minding responsibilities in the family while his wife went out. He also took to drinking quite heavily as a means of relieving his feelings.

For reasons that still remain not altogether clear, although a degree of sexual interest in young females emerged as a possible factor, sexual contact between David and his older daughter began to occur, particularly when he was feeling most lacking in self esteem and when his self pity was at a peak. These feelings also coincided with periods of heavy drinking, which appeared to have had a disinhibiting affect on his inclinations to offend against his daughter.

Although there had always been a strong bond of affection between David and his older daughter, his commission of the offences against her led to him experiencing anger and disgust towards himself, which to a degree it seemed, he projected onto his daughter. He sought no help with the situation until the offences came to light following a family dispute unconnected with the sexual abuse, and at the time he was first seen he tended to rationalise responsibility for the offences away from himself and onto his wife and daughter.

In line with the principles outlined earlier, psychological intervention with David took place in the context of multi-disciplinary involvement with all members of the family. A social worker had particular responsibility for helping and supporting David's wife while another social worker and a psychiatrist related particularly to the children of the family. Psychological treatment for David was the particular responsibility of the clinical psychologist (author) in collaboration with his probation officer.

The context of these linked interventions was a probation order for David in which he was initially required to live away from the family home, reconciliation with the family only taking place in gradual steps as progress in treatment was effected. Developments with the family were monitored through multi-disciplinary case conferences which looked at progress with marital therapy for the couple, individual counselling for David and counselling for the children, together with questions of risk to the children represented by each stage in the reconciliation process.

After two and a half years the family were successfully reunited, this being the outcome which each member of the family had sought, and their continuing progress continued to be monitored by the social workers and clinical psychologist.

CONCLUSION

Sex offending is a problem which has been with society, and will doubtless continue to be so for very many years. Its manifestations range from the violent rapes and murders which make headline news, through the persistent, sexually-motivated acts of indecent exposure, voyeurism and obscene telephone calls, into the cultural and sub-cultural norms of society as a whole.

Women and children are the most likely victims of sexual offending and men the most likely perpetrators. Our sexual attitudes and behaviours as a society form the context for sexual offending, within which the pre-dispositions of specific individuals, possibly victimised themselves as children, interact with the specitic situations in which offences typically occur.

146

Criminal statistics indicate that, while the reported instances of most sexual offences have remained fairly stable over recent years, some offences, notably rape, are being reported at an alarmingly escalating rate. A policy of combining action for individuals (help for victims and treatment and/or control of offenders) with changes in social policy (equal opportunities in education and employment, re-dressing inaccurate or distorted media depictions or the sexes, and so on) is perhaps the most fruitful way ahead.

References

1. Tutt, N. Personal Communication. 1986.

2. Perkins, D.E. 'Psychological Treatment of Offenders in Prison and the Community'. In Williams, T., Alves, E. & Shapland, J. (Eds.) *Options for the Mentally Abnormal Offender*. Issues in Criminological and Legal Psychology, Number 6. The British Psychological Society, Leicester, 1984.

3. Abel, G.G. & Blanchard, E.B. 'The Role of Fantasy in the Treatment of Sexual Deviation' *Archives of General Psychiatry*. 30, 1974, 467-475.

4. Finkelhor, D. *Child Sex Abuse. New Therapy and Research*. Free Press, New York, 1984.

5. Elliott, M. *Preventing Child Sexual Assault*. Vigo Press Ltd, London, 1985.

6. Robertson, D. Personal communication, 1986.

7. Tucker, N. 'A Panic over Child Sexual Abuse' *New Scientist*. 18 October, 1985.

8. Finkelhor, D. *Sexually Victimised Children*. Free Press, New York, 1979.

9. British Association for the Study and Prevention of Child Abuse. *Child Sexual Abuse*. BASPCAN, London, 1980.

10. Gittleson, N.L., Eacott, S.E. & Mehta, B.M. 'Victims of Indecent Exposure' *British Journal of Psychiatry*. 132, 1978, 61-66.

11. Perkins, D.E. 'The Treatment of Sex Offenders'. In Feldman, M.P. (Ed.) *Developments in the Study of Criminal Behaviour*. Vol 1. Wiley, Chichester, 1982.

12. Perkins, D.E. (In Press). 'A Psychological Treatment Programme for Sex Offenders'. In McGurk, B.J. (Ed.) *Applying Psychology to Imprisonment*. NFER.

13. Renvoise, J. *Incest: A Family Pattern*. Routledge and Kegan Paul, London, 1982.

14. Reifen, D. 'Court Procedures in Israel to Protect Child-Victims of Sexual Assaults'. In Drapkin, I. & Ciano, E. (Eds) *Victimology: A New Focus*. Vol. 3. D.C. Heath, Lexington, Mass., 1973.

15. Giaretto, H. 'Humanistic Treatment of Father-Daughter Incest'. In Schultz, L.G. (Ed.) *The Sexual Victimology of Youth*. Charles G. Thomas, Springfield, Illinois, 1980.

16. CIBA Foundation. Child Sexual Abuse Within the Family. Ponter, R. (Ed.). Tavistock, London, 1984.

17. Freund, K., 'Diagnosing Heterosexual Pedophilia by Means of a Test for Sexual Interest' *Behaviour Research and Therapy*. 3, 1965, 229-234.

18. Freund, K. 'Erotic Preferences in Pedophilia' *Behaviour Research and Therapy*. 5, 1967, 339-348.

19. Abel, G.G., Blanchard, E.B., Barlow, D.H. & Mavissakalian, M. 'Identifying Specific Erotic Cues in Sexual Deviations by Audio-Taped Descriptions' *Journal of Applied Behavioural Analysis*. 8, 1975, 58-71.

20. Abel, G.G., Becker, J.V., Blanchard, E.B. & Djenderedjian, A. 'Differentiating Sexual Aggressiveness with Penile Measures' *Criminal Justice and Behaviour*. 5, 1978, 315-332.

21. Matthews, R. *Assessment of Sexual Offenders at Wormwood Scrubs*. Paper presented at annual conference of the British Psychological Society, Exeter, 1977.

22. Barlow, D.H., Leitenberg, H. & Agras, W.S. 'The Experimental Control of Sexual Deviation Through Manipulation of the Noxious Scene in Covert Sensitization' *Journal of Abnormal Psychology*. 74, 1969, 596-601.

23. Serber, M. & Wolpe, J. 'Behaviour Therapy Techniques'. In Resnick, H.L.P. & Wolfgang, M.E. (Eds) *Sexual Behaviours*. Little Brown, Boston, 1972.

24. Callahan, E.J. & Leitenberg, H. 'Aversion Therapy for Sexual Deviation: Contingent Shock and Covert Sensitisation' *Journal of Abnormal Psychology*. 81, 1973, 60-73.

25. Abel, G.G., Blanchard, E.B. & Becker, J.V. 'Psychological Treatment of Rapists'. In Walker, M.J. & Brodsky, S.L. (Eds) *Sexual Assault*. Lexington Books, Lexington, Mass., 1976.

26. Crawford, D.A. & Allen, J.V. 'A Social Skills Training Programme with Sex Offenders'. In Cook, M. & Wilson, G. (Eds) *Love and Attraction: Proceedings of an International Conference*. Pergamon, Oxford, 1979.

27. Meichenbaum, D. 'Cognitive Behaviour Modification'. In Spence, J.T., Carlson, R.C. & Thibaut, J.W. (Eds) *Behavioural Approaches to Therapies*. General Learning Press, New York, 1976.

28. Crawford, D.A. 'Treatment Approaches with Paedophiles'. In Howells, K. & Cook, M. (Eds) *Adult Sexual Interest in Children*. Academic Press, London, 1981.

The Sex Offender Treatment Program: An Evaluative Overview

Ann Fillmore and Coralie Jewell

INTRODUCTION: THE NECESSITY FOR SEX OFFENDER TREATMENT PROGRAMS

Sexual offenders produce victims; a high percentage of sex offenders were themselves victims as young boys – 60-80 per cent. A high percentage of prostitutes (95 per cent), both male and female, were victims of early childhood sexual molestation. Although all victims of sexual molestation do not become offenders, all victims are affected in their emotional development, their ability to form personal relationships, and to provide a safe, non-abusive environment for their own children.

There is some question as to whether or not adult sex offenders, either male or female, can be 'cured' of their sexual addiction; but there is no doubt that those offenders who complete a program such as the one at the Center for Behavioral Intervention in Portland, Oregon, or Northwest Treatment Associates in Seattle, Washington, rarely recidivate. As for juvenile sex offenders, the necessity for treatment programs is, in a sense, even more imperative. Nicholas Groth, author of *Men Who Rape* [1], wrote:

> 'The thing that I am struck by is how often the behavior of the adult sex offender is already there in the juvenile offender. Rather than dismissing the sexual misbehavior of the juvenile offender as adolescent mischief, the boy should be carefully and competently evaluated. Clinical services need to be provided for this target population. Neglect doesn't solve the problem.'

There is ample evidence that teenagers can be successfully treated and can be returned safely to the community. This obviously means a tremendous saving for the public in both human and financial terms.

> 'Annual per-client cost in a specialised sex-offender community-based

treatment program in New York, for instance, is approximately $500 per year. The annual cost to incarcerate one juvenile in a secure Division for Youth facility is approximately $80,000. Thus, fiscally, we cannot afford *not* to provide early remedies, nor can we afford it for safety reasons' [2].

OVERVIEW

The *Preliminary Report on 1985 Nationwide Survey of U.S. Juvenile and Adult Sex Offender Treatment Programs and Providers* [3] presented by Fay Honey Knopp of PREAP, gives a comprehensive look at the current trends in sex offender treatment programming.

'During the last decade', writes Ms. Knopp, 'our files mushroomed from 20 identified programs to approximately 600 specialised treatment services for juvenile/adolescent and adult sex offenders. These figures do not include: 1) those programs that treat the incest offender only in the context of incest family; 2) programs that treat the sex offender in nonspecialised groups; or 3) the burgeoning 'self-help' movement.' [4]

This PREAP survey of the existing sex offender treatment programs used questionnaires containing 23 fields of information which went into their computerised data base. The following is a summary of the results [3]:

'1. Specialised assessment and treatment of juvenile and adult sex offenders is growing rapidly.

2. It can be said with deep concern that its growth is not guided by any systematic development or testing of treatment approaches and outcomes.

3. It can be reported with some amazement that training for this discipline is only rarely integrated into the formal curricula of institutions of higher education that train our professionals. Instead, information is exchanged and treatment techniques are advanced largely through informal networks, occasional conferences and sporadic training sessions.

4. Distribution of services is very uneven. Some criminal justice systems and legislators behave as though there were no remedies for this population and sentences (in the court) particularly of older adolescents and adults, are climbing upward.'

Some states (in the USA) have no juvenile programs, others have only one or two. Most programs for youthful sex offenders are in Washington, Oregon, California and Minnesota. Five states do not have services for adult sex offenders at all.

There were 188 community-based providers and 82 residential, and the summary of the kind of programs they offered is:

> group therapy – 91 per cent
> family therapy – 80 per cent
> behavioral methods – 63 per cent use such methods as covert sensitisation, masturbatory satiation and cognitive rehearsal and 35 per cent use aversive conditioning, mostly olfactory
> penile transducer – 31.3 per cent
> Depo-Provera – 18 per cent
> 'thinking errors' – 42 per cent

The responding juvenile programs were only slightly different:

> group therapy – 86 per cent
> family therapy – 90 per cent
> behavioral methods – 52 per cent mostly covert sensitisation and cognitive conditioning and only 19.8 per cent use aversive conditioning
> penile transducer – 14 per cent
> Depo-Provera – 6 per cent
> 'thinking errors' – 38 per cent

Some programs treated female sex offenders, mostly in separate groups; a very few programs had special groups and curricula for developmentally disabled and low functioning offenders in either the adult or juvenile category, although a large number of programs (69 per cent) did have facilities in order to work also with victims [3].

THE CENTER FOR BEHAVIORAL INTERVENTION, PORTLAND, OREGON, USA

The majority of programs use several methodologies in tandem; for example, behavioral therapy, group and family therapy and the most successful ones combine these modalities with aversion conditioning and physiological assessment using the penile plethysmograph, or penile transducer. The Center for Behavioral Intervention in Portland, Oregon, USA – which was one of the programs surveyed, can be used as an example of the latter to explain what happens as the offender actually goes through the treatment program.

The Center for Behavioral Intervention has a comprehensive out-patient assessment and treatment program and uses a philosophy with components of both psychological and behavioral learning theory to explain the causative factors precipitating sexual offences which are undeniably multiple and complex. Although it is an outpatient program, it maintains a highly structured environment for its patients, as well as high expectations. The offender is made well aware that the primary goal of treatment is protection of the community and that in order to provide that safety, rigid rules of behavior must be kept, the treatment and therapy regimen must be adhered to and all safeguards available to ensure such compliance will be used. One necessary ingredient to back up such demands is that the offender is court mandated into the program which means all the personnel involved keep in close contact with and have the understanding and support that is essential from the probation departments [5].

Assessment and Evaluation Procedures

In order to provide a thorough evaluation of the offender as he first comes into the legal system, a multi-faceted assessment approach is used by the Center for Behavioral Intervention which includes: reviewing pertinent records, police reports, victim/s' statement/s; obtaining a social and sexual history, a spouse's statement; administering an array of psychological tests and questionnaires; and performing a physiological examination using the penile plethysmograph. This latter provides a unique and necessary treatment component regarding the offender's sexual arousal response to various stimuli that have the potential of eliciting unwanted and illegal overt behaviors [6].

Such an examination consists of, first, a brief interview with the therapist and signing a consent form. The offender then enters a private room and attaches a penile transducer to his penis, after which he is presented with a number of erotic slides depicting both male and female, very young children, pre-adolescent children, adolescent children and adults. Next, he listens to several audio tapes which depict sexual behavior with the above-mentioned age groups and involve various themes such as consenting sexual intercourse, coercive sexual intercourse and rape. Responses are recorded on a chart recorder and compared to statistical standardised responses known for sexual deviants and normals. All the data are correlated and analysed, and a detailed plan is formulated including specific recommendations as to the placement of the individual. It may be found that the offender is so disturbed that a secure facility is the only option. Otherwise, he is referred and remanded into the outpatient program at the Centre for Behavioral Intervention [5].

The offender is required to take complete responsibility for his deviant behavior and must recognise the need for treatment. He must be willing to spend a significant amount of time modifying his behavioral patterns and he must work at resolving his legal problems through the court. Of course, he must be motivated.

Even with the pressure of the court behind him, the process is by no means easy for a sex offender to accomplish. Not only does it mean that a large part of his formerly free time will be spent working on intense introspection and often painful change processes, but there is also the fact that the restrictions such as not being around children except under very strictly supervised conditions can mean a complete change of profession might be necessary. It is not unknown for child molesters to seek out job positions that enable them to have access to children. Naturally, what close supervision means at home or during visits at home (which comes much later in the treatment process) is that the offender can no longer be alone with his own children, not even be able to sit next to the child in the car, or do many of the other activities that a father (or mother) might naturally do.

Although during the initial judicial proceedings, the abuser is unable to deny the social unacceptability of his behavior and may exhibit extreme remorse (mostly due to the fact that he was caught), this discomfort is usually short-lived. Most sexual abusers have built up a remarkable denial system which enables them to construct amazing cognitive distortions to cover their crimes. Common explanations for the molestation are: 'I was providing her with sex education' (speaking of the molestation of a five-year-old neighbour's daughter) or that 'she seduced me by wearing such a flimsy nightdress' (said of a four-year-old sister of a sixteen-year-old offender) or 'he had an erection when I tickled him, so I thought he'd want to get it off' (a comment of a father about the molestation of his infant son which continued for five years after this initial episode). Thus it is obvious that internal motivation by itself is not enough to maintain the abuser in a rigorous treatment program that requires a major modification in his lifestyle.

Most therapists who have dealt with the sex offender population for any length of time have learned that the skills and knowledge they were provided with in their formal education in mental health do not apply when working with sex offenders. In fact, the very skills that make many of us excellent therapists in marital, family or individual therapy do more damage than good when employed with sex offenders. A classic example is the expected transference between patient and therapist; the sex offender is a very skilful imitator and manipulator and can take on the smallest behaviors of his therapist but use them only to cover the yet existing deviancies.

It is extremely important that therapists in this field have a keen sense that their own value system is a healthy, intact, and realistic one that can be used directly in confronting the offender's distorted perceptions. The therapist must be highly sceptical, confrontive, directive and well-trained in the dynamics and treatment of sexual deviancy. Being well read in the area is essential (a list has been provided as a bibliography). If at all possible, the therapist should be trained by a professional who has him/herself assessed and treated large numbers of offenders. Many people are easily misled into becoming offender advocates instead of community advocates since offenders are notorious for seducing therapists (and court personnel and anyone else they come in contact with) into feeling sympathetic towards them, thus creating more victims as they go. Thus, the need for intermittent physiological assessment and to constantly remember that sexual deviancy is similar to other addictions that must be viewed as incurable but not untreatable [5].

The Individualised Behavioral Program

One of the earliest steps employed to assess motivation for change is the arranging of a contractual agreement between the client, therapist and legal agencies. This contract clearly stipulates that the abuser will participate in a treatment program for a minimum of one year and lists goals to be accomplished through treatment.

Prior to entering the group therapy program, each client participates in an individualised behavioural program. During weekly meetings, the client works on eradicating compulsive deviant sexual arousal which he may be secretly reinforcing through masturbation and fantasy. The Director of the Center for Behavioral Intervention, Steven H. Jensen, developed an olfactory aversion method called Minimal Arousal Conditioning which has proved to be quite effective in reducing deviant arousal [5].

The client puts together a written description of one of his most arousing sexual involvements with one of his victims. He is then assessed on the plethysmograph while reading the descriptions aloud. The technician notes at what point in the description the client begins to have minimal arousal (5 per cent). The client is then instructed in the methods of pairing aversive conditioning (olfactory aversion using ammonia) with his reaction. The offender is to practice the aversive procedure nightly as homework sessions and keep track of his reactions on a behavior chart. The process usually lasts about ten weeks or until he can demonstrate to the technician that his deviant arousal is under 5 per cent [5].

Covert sensitisation is begun once this happens, meaning he pairs descriptions of deviant behavior with an aversive fantasy. This is also practised as homework and checked with the plethysmograph in the office. Also during the first ten weeks, he learns to recognise his cognitive distortions which are analysed and disputed by the therapist until the offender is able to give accurate self-statements to counter the old beliefs he used which permitted him to molest.

The offender should feel rewarded by the changes he experiences in himself and with encouragement he can face the next challenge: group therapy for himself and, if appropriate, his spouse.

Group Therapy

During the first two months of this section of the treatment, the client is required to write an extensive autobiography in which he must identify the patterns influencing his development of deviant behavior. He must state accurately his entire sexual history. In group, the other members often confront each other about the completeness of the document and since they are all very aware of their own propensity to falsify their history and the extent of their offences, the results are always emotional and often surprising. In addition, each offender does an 'offender's development chart' which furthers his understanding of what influences in his life precipitated the aberrant sexual behaviors.

Also in group, the victim's descriptions in the police reports of the alleged sexual activities are read aloiud. Here must be pointed out the great benefit of having police officers who are skilled at interviewing victims and thorough about taking down all the details possible. In every sex offender treatment group surveyed, the victim/s' statements have been proved to be 95 per cent accurate, their only fault being that very often the victim has not been able to tell the whole victimisation story to the police or to the court for one reason or another. The remainder of the victim's history is likely to come out under the scrutiny of the other group members and is extremely valuable as a lesson in reality for the offender. His eventual self-disclosure is an important step in learning to accept responsibility for his actions, past and present.

Discussion of what happened in group proceeds with other family members, along with discussion of his fear of rejection. The reactions of the family members are brought back to the men's group and sometimes re-enacted during the meetings.

The offenders begin to internalise the concept of total responsibility for their deviant behavior and recognise that there are similar identifiable patterns of deviant behavior. As these insights occur, the group members recognise the need for behavioral change on their part. They work out a *Deviant Behavioral Cycle* which is shared with group and family members with the intent that these others will help identify the precipitating events and behavior and intervene long before the deviant behavior begins to reoccur. The sexual abuser often experiences great difficulty in sensing when he is entering the upswing of his cycle and is heading for trouble; whereas, the people around him, if trained, can usually spot it immediately.

The abuser's unrealistic expectations, irrational beliefs and perceived rejections are assessed and confronted in conjunction with the cycle, as are the old cognitive distortions that allowed him to rationalise coercive, assaultive, and aberrant sexual behavior. Some clinicians hypothesise that these cognitive distortions are one of the more important factors enabling the offender to continue his deviancy [1,5,7,8,9].

Since the sexual abuser is characterised as a socially immature individual and often displays numerous deficits in his social skills, communication and social skills training are an important part of group activity. Knowledge of how to converse, ask open-ended questions, maintain eye contact, gauge appropriate self-disclosure, actively listen, and give or receive compliments becomes an integral part of treatment. Not too surprisingly, these men have little knowledge of how to employ a variety of heterosexual dating skills, including asking a woman for a date, enjoying recreational activities and appreciating affection for a woman, touching and sensitivity in sex, and the technical aspects of sexual arousal. An effective group leader must both identify and train individuals in these specific skills. Many offenders and their wives have sexually dysfunctional relationships which have in part contributed to the molestation or rape. It is imperative that sexuality be an integral part of both the men's and couples' groups. With proper training the offender can more effectively discuss his sexual needs and meet the expectations – being developed in the wives' group being run alongside theirs – of his adult partner. Rarely do men molest children when they are satisfied in their primary sexual relationship with a spouse; thus it is required that the couple improve their sexual relationship even though they may feel it is flawless.

There are reading assignments and discussions of each topic, and the social skills are practised through behavioral rehearsal exercises. As each skill is acquired, the offender notes it on specially designed forms which contain information about the time, date, frequency, setting, and outcome. The results are charted weekly on a group bulletin board so that each member can monitor the behavioral successes of other members. Briefly, the various skills include, but are not limited to:

> communication skills
> assertiveness training
> anger management
> cognitive restructuring
> dating skills
> sexual skills training
> recreational skills
> stress management
> empathy training [10]

Materials

This behavioral group program has utilised five primary books as well as a number of chapters and articles. The first book, *Male Sexuality* [11] dispels certain sexual myths and reviews a number of sensible components regarding normal sexual functioning. The second book, *Your Perfect Right* [12] discusses assertiveness training and open communication skills. It uses a model for those group members who need to develop spontaneous and fluent communication skills. The third book, *The New Guide to Rational Living* [13] serves to help the group members assess their self-talk and teaches how specific cognitive messages can maintain deviant or non-productive behavior. *The Sexual Addiction* [14] examines the etiology of sexual compulsiveness and the belief systems that support addiction, as well as covering the family system as a contributing factor in sexual abuse. The fifth book, *Agress-Less* [15], is a step-by-step approach to conflict resolution, aggression management, and positive skills building. Also used in group are a variety of articles, audio-visual materials, and films.

Since treatment is a long-term program, lasting at least one year, this approach ensures the habituation of appropriate recreational, social and leisure activities as well as a constant monitoring of sexual behavior. Before the abuser is discharged, he is required to submit a plan which outlines his employment goals, recreational activities, avocational pursuits, his methods to avoid deviant arousal patterns, and guidelines for proper behavior [5,9,16].

In addition to adhering to his maintenance program, the offender is encouraged to attend follow-up meetings. Treatment is open-ended and on-going, and group sessions are always available, especially when the offender feels the need to get further encouragement [5,9,16].

Marital-Sexual Enhancement Meetings – Couples Groups

Sexual abusers with committed partners attend a second weekly group meeting to accomplish these goals:

1. to better educate the spouse regarding her husband's aberrant behavior

2. discuss effective ways to resolve their sexual/marital problems

3. improve the quality of their sexual relationship

4. enable the partner to identify and intervene in her husband's deviant cycle

5. build communication, problem solving and relationship skills.

The first major problem facing the therapist during these meetings is the spouse's denial and minimisation of her husband's deviant behavior. In many cases, the husband has led his wife to believe that the criminal charges are grossly inaccurate and/or overstated. The wife often reinforces her husband's distorted perceptions and unwittingly undermines the treatment program. Consequently, the spouse's distorted perceptions are first reviewed and a detailed explanation of her husband's behavior is given [6,17,18,19].

Both must develop higher levels of self-esteem and explore their developmental history in detail, with emphasis on their values, role expectations, child rearing practices, beliefs and support systems and sexual history. There should be an understanding on both partners' behalf that this is a life-long problem, which will always have to be monitored.

Graduation

Clients are graduated only when there is agreement from the men's group, the couple's group, the therapist and the probation officer. Graduation is followed by decreased participation, monthly attendance in both groups for four months, then once after three months, six months and then back after a year. Physiological assessments accompany the follow-up treatment plan on much the same basis [5].

Juvenile Groups

Juvenile offenders (12-18 years old) are dealt with in much the same way, the only major differences being that family therapy replaces the marital-sexual/couples groups. Parents groups are run simultaneously to examine their misperceptions and cognitive distortions regarding their son's (daughter's) deviant behavior [3,4,8,20].

To date, this program has proved extremely effective. With continued research its modalities of treatment and various components will become even more refined and more widely used.

Many more comprehensive programs like the one at the Centre for Behavioral Intervention are needed both in the United States and Europe. For more information regarding programs in the United States, contact:

> Fay Honey Knopp
> Prison Research Education Action Projects
> Shoreham Depot Road
> Orwell, Vermont, USA 05780

or

> Steven H. Jensen, Director
> Center for Behavioral Intervention
> 4560 S.W. 110th
> Beaverton, Oregon, USA 97005

and in the U.K.:

> Dr Rosemary Wool
> HM Prison Service
> Cleland House
> Page Street
> London SW1P 4LN

References

1. Groth, A.N. *Men Who Rape*. Plenum Press, New York, 1979.

2. Knopp, F.H. *The Youthful Sex Offender: The Rationale and Goals of Early Intervention and Treatment*. Safer Society Press, Syracuse, N.Y., 1985.

3. Knopp, F.H. *Preliminary Report on 1985 Nationwide Survey of U.S. Juvenile and Adult Sex Offender Treatment Programs and Providers*. PREAP, Tampa, Fla., 1986.

4. Knopp, F.H., Rosenberg, J. & Stevenson, W. *Report on Nationwide Survey of Juvenile and Adult Sex Offender Treatment Programs and Providers*. PREAP, Syracuse, N.Y., 1986.

5. Jensen, S. Center for Behavioral Intervention. Private papers.

6. McGovern, K. & Jensen, S. 'Behavioral Group Treatment Methods for Sexual Disorders and Dysfunctions'. In Upper, D. and Ross, S. *Handbook of Behavioral Group Therapy*. Plenum Press, New York, 1985.

7. Finkelhor, D. *Child Sexual Abuse*. Free Press, New York, 1984.

8. Knopp, F.H. *Remedial Intervention in Adolescent Sex Offenses: Nine Program Descriptions*. Safer Society Press, Syracuse, N.Y., 1982.

9. Knopp, F.H. *Retraining Adult Sex Offenders: Methods and Models*. Safer Society Press, Syracuse, N.Y., 1984.

10. Jensen, S., Fillmore, A. and Jewell, C. *Evaluation and Treatment of the Adolescent Sex Offender*. Westridge Publishers, Portland, OR., 1986.

11. Zilbergeld, B. *Male Sexuality*. Bantam Books, Toronto, 1978.

12. Alberti & Emmons *Your Perfect Right*. Impact Publishers, 1970.

13. Ellis, A. & Harper *The New Guide to Rational Living*. Wilshire Book Company, 1974.

14. Carnes, P. *Out of the Shadows: Understanding Sexual Addiction*. CompCare, Minneapolis, MN., 1983.

15. Goldstein, A.P. & Rosenbaum, A. *Aggress-Less*. Prentice-Hall Inc., Englewood Cliffs, N.J., 1982.

16. Marques, J.K., Pithers, W.D. & Marlatt, G.A. *Relapse Prevention: A Self-Control Program for Sex Offenders*. Unpublished papers.

17. Mayer, A. *Incest: A Treatment Manual for Therapy with Victims, Spouses and Offenders*. Learning Publications, Inc., Holmes Beach, Fla., 1983.

18 Finkelhor, D., Gelles, R.J., Hotaling, G.T. & Straus, M.A. *The Dark Side of Families: Current Family Violence Research*. Sage Publishers, Beverly Hills, CA., 1983.

19. Herman, J. *Father-Daughter Incest*. Harvard University Press, Cambridge, MA., 1981.

20. Porter, E. *Treating the Young Male Victim of Sexual Assault: Issues and Intervention Strategies*. Safer Society Press, Syracuse, N.Y., 1986.

Additional References

1. Abel, G.G. 'The Components of Rapists' Sexual Arousal' *Archives of General Psychiatry*. 34, 1977, 895-903.

2. Annon, J.S. *The Behavioral Treatment of Sexual Problems*. Enabling Systems, Inc., Honolulu, HI., 1976.

3. Burgess, A.W., Groth, A.N., Holstrom, L.L. & Sgroi, S.M. *Sexual Assault of Children and Adolescents*. Lexington Books, Lexington, MA., 1978.

4. Cox, D.J. & Diatzman, R.J. *Exhibitionism: Description, Assessment, and Treatment*. Garland Press, New York, 1980.

5. Finkelhor, D. *Sexually Victimised Children*. The Free Press, New York, 1979.

6. Greer, J.G. & Stuart, I.R. *The Sexual Aggressor*. Van Nostrand Reinhold Co., 1983.

7. Madaras, L. *What's Happening to My Body? Book for Boys*. Newmarket Press, New York, 1984.

8. Rada, R.T. *Clinical Aspects of the Rapist*. Grune & Stratton, New York, 1978.

9. Samenow, S.E. & Yochelson, S. *The Criminal Personality*. Vol. I & II. Jason Aronson, New York, 1977.

10. Sgroi, S.M. *Handbook of Clinical Intervention in Child Sexual Abuse*. Lexington Books, Lexington, MA., 1985.

11. USDHHS *Sexual Abuse of Children: Selected Readings*. DHHS, Washington, D.C., 1980.

Responding to AIDS: Practice and Policy

Reg Vernon

INTRODUCTION

This paper looks at the various problems which may arise in clients as a consequence of infection with Human Immunosuppressive Virus (HIV, otherwise known as HTLV III) [1]. A basic assumption is that the ordinary skills possessed by any social worker are sufficient to deal with such clients but that there are certain issues arising from the condition which are not self-evident and may pose problems when helping [2]. A dominant issue is that the disease has become, probably inextricably, linked with male homosexuality. Clearly, the disease is not confined to homosexual men. For present purposes, however, I have chosen to concentrate on this group of sufferers, and the male pronoun is used throughout.

At present, in non-third world countries, AIDS is a disease which affects mainly homosexual/bisexual men, intravenous drug users who share needles, and haemophiliacs. The gay plague image has become dominant, and this has unleashed a remarkable wave of 'homophobia', especially (but not exclusively) in the popular press. There is some reason to believe that social workers are also susceptible to these homophobic reactions which may adversely affect their practice. Social work has concentrated particularly strongly on the conventional heterosexual family, somewhat to the detriment of other units, and there is certainly very little about homosexual lifestyles in social work literature [3]. De Crescenjas and McGill [4] found in America that social workers were the most homophobic of mental health workers with 43 per cent showing a homophobic response. Yet figures indicate that, on a fairly conservative estimate, if a social worker has 100 people in his caseload in a year he will have met around ten exclusive homosexuals and another 10-20 with significant homosexual experience [5]. Many social workers, though, would be hard pressed to identify a handful of gay clients in a career, so by viewing society from a heterosexist viewpoint considerable disservice is being done to a significant minority of clients [6]. This also means that the potential for conflict between a social worker making heterosexist assumptions and a gay client is great, although it does not mean that a gay social worker will handle a gay client better, and a repressed gay helper might be totally incapacitated.

Sexuality is not fixed or given, changing according to culture and time, and its expression in an individual can vary over that person's life [7]. Therefore, before dealing with any persons with AIDS or a related condition, the social worker ought to examine his attitudes to homosexuality, if only because any contact with the voluntary support groups involved with people with AIDS means almost certain contact with homosexuals. There are a number of relatively simple ways in which the individual can explore his attitudes to homosexuality and begin to correct them. This may be done by, firstly, looking at one's background and history, early attitudes to gays and any gays one has known, and examining one's feelings about same sex affection and eroticism. Secondly, it is now much easier to learn the facts about homosexuality with the wide range of literature fairly readily available [8]. Thirdly, research has demonstrated that getting to know lesbians and gay men is an invaluable antidote to homophobia.

Messing et al. [9] consider that there are some homophobic responses which are the peculiar vice of social workers, although they are probably often used unconsciously. Denial is a primary manifestation: statistics about the large number of gays are denied as exaggerated by the individual who believes the heterosexual family to be the only valid lifestyle. A common reaction among educated people with a liberal world view is that sexual orientation does not matter, but this ignores the fact that, for many gays, orientation has had a profound effect upon their lives and must be taken into account when this is appropriate. Hostility is a form of homophobia which can lead the helper to try to 'convert' the gay person as a hidden agenda, which makes the interaction baffling for the client who may then develop a contempt for the helper. To exaggerate the significance of orientation and to treat it instead of the presenting problem, constitutes a homophobic reaction.

THE SOCIAL WORK MANAGEMENT OF CLIENTS WITH AIDS

Testing for HIV Positivity

This is in the form of blood tests which indicate the presence of antibodies to the HIV. The tests available at present, however, do not test directly for the virus. The presence of antibodies does not indicate whether the virus is still present, and a negative result does not necessarily mean that the virus is *not* present since it may take some time for antibodies to be detected and re-testing must be carried out later. So being HIV positive does not mean that AIDS will automatically develop; this is only occurring in about 10-20 per cent of positives at present. There may also be other strains of the virus not properly detectable with current tests. Because of these problems with testing and with fears about the confidentiality of test results, there has been controversy surrounding this issue [10] which is not yet resolved and which the social worker should bear in mind if counselling someone about taking the test. Miller [11] suggests guidelines for this process. Before the test, there should be a detailed counselling session on the consequences of being found HIV positive for, e.g. life insurance, mortgage, job. The anxieties which surround these are discussed and the person is left to think about them before a decision is reached [12].

After the test, if the person is found positive, Miller suggests the following:-

(1) He is allowed to ventilate;
(2) Counselling is given on safer sex [13];
(3) The person is given a phone number to use at any time;
(4) He is asked not to tell anyone immediately unless a lover knows he has taken the test;
(5) He is asked to think about who ought to know and to return to discuss this;
(6) He is screened for psychiatric disturbance; and
(7) Necessary follow-up takes place.

If the person proves negative it is probably wise to ensure he is aware of safer sex practices. It is obviously essential that the helper is able to discuss aspects of sexuality, including gay sexuality, without discomfort.

Psychological Conditions to which Clients with AIDS are Liable

The helper needs, principally, to look out for anxiety, depression, obsessional behaviour and agitated uncertainty, all conditions with which social workers will be familiar. Green [14] discusses them in some detail, but here only two require further comment. Anxiety is obviously a factor in anyone who is, or feels he is, infected, but it can confound the diagnosis, since the early symptoms of HIV infection (AIDS) and anxiety are very similar. For example, vomiting and diarrhoea, lethargy, night sweats and weight loss are among common symptoms. Thus care has to be taken to distinguish genuinely infected people from the worried well. Uncertainty is linked with anxiety and it is seen as one of the most debilitating aspects of early diagnosis and should not be underestimated. A compelling reason for being alert to these emotions is that there is convincing evidence that stress suppresses the immune system.

CATEGORIES OF AIDS CLIENTS

For convenience, and to bring out the special problems, the following categories have been used. These broadly correspond to those used in the available literature.

(1) Those with frank AIDS.
(2) Those with HIV related illnesses and persistent generalised lymphadeno-pathy.
(3) Asymptomatic HIV seropositives.
(4) Those concerned to reduce their risk of acquiring AIDS: the worried well.
(5) Those with pre-senile dementia and mental conditions associated with HIV virus.
(6) Intra-venous drug users.
(7) Haemophiliacs.
(8) Pregnant mothers and foetae.
(9) Heterosexuals as a group.
(10) The lovers, family and friends of the diagnosed.

(1) *Those with Frank AIDS*

The social worker in this situation will probably be in the hospital setting, although fieldworkers may become involved as a result of referral from the hospital for a patient going home or by the client for help and services, as is increasingly the case.

The client needs to be helped to deal with his diagnosis. It may not be a surprise but hopes may have been built up during investigation. Therefore, he needs help to come to terms with his diagnosis, both emotionally and intellectually. He may have questions about the illness that need to be answered in a straightforward and frank way; this is absolutely essential to proper, effective counselling, since advice will have to be given on safe sex practices, and if the client does not believe the helper he will not carry these out. It is important that the social worker should have close contact with the doctor in charge of the client [15].

Clients in this category will be facing death and this is an important aspect of the work with this group. Ordinarily when dealing with a dying client the social worker may have in mind the different stages of dying given by Kubler-Ross [16]. Miller [15] considers these to be still useful at the end stage, but because of the time scale (up to three years from diagnosis to death) he has provided a list of qualitative issues which take into account the particular problems of AIDS clients. They are:

(1) Shock of diagnosis and facing possible death.
(2) Feelings of powerlessness to change circumstances with consequent frustration and anger.
(3) Reduced physical functioning because of declining health.
(4) Anxiety about the reactions of others, with consequent social withdrawal and loss of social support.
(5) Reduced cognitive functioning because of anxiety, depression, obsessional worries and possible intellectual impairment.
(6) Reduced sexual functioning, loss of libido and erectile dysfunction.
(7) Fear of infecting others, particularly lovers.
(8) Concern about the lover and how he/she can cope.
(9) Fear of being deserted and dying alone.
(10) Fear of dying in pain and discomfort.
(11) Social, domestic and occupational disruption.

This list addresses sexual aspects which cannot be avoided. It is important for the helper to assess how the client is reacting to the diagnosis and as soon as possible help the client to regain a feeling of control over his life; he will also have many practical tasks involved in settling his affairs. A gay man may be in contact with his family but not known to be gay; 'coming out' to one's close family is a stressful event at the best of times, but to do this and reveal the diagnosis compounds the problem. Some may opt to move away from their family and thus increase their isolation.

Lopez and Getzel [17] describe a method of supporting a person with AIDS during the last stages of his life. This has been used by the Gay Men's Health Crisis in New York. The approach is first to attend to the emotional and specific material needs of the client and then provide social support in collaboration with family and friends. The financial side may not be so important in this country but is a source of acute anxiety in America as insurance begins to run out. Lopez and Getyel outline the following phases:

Phase 1. Engagement and Assessment. The gay AIDS client has not perhaps been dependent and may find this depressing. Initially, the worker engages the client in a non-confrontational manner, allowing for emotional expression; often, powerful feelings are masked by denial. The worker assists with management but vigilantly seeks to maximise the patient's control and choices.

Phase 2. Assisting and supporting, while preserving autonomy. It is easy for the worker to set back this phase by pre-empting the client's autonomy because of anxiety over his deteriorating condition, thus contributing to the client's sense of powerlessness and depression. At the same time, the worker must on occasion explore and respond to the client's covert and ambivalent requests for help.

Phase 3. Explaining the relationship, and the meaning of AIDS. As trust develops between the client and worker it is not unusual for the client to question the worker's motivation. This type of exchange reflects the client's doubts about the worker's acceptance of him and his health condition. The client may pick up the worker's fear of AIDS, and covertly express envy and rage about the worker's health as his illness grows worse.

Phase 4. Supporting the client's indirect recognition of death. During the decline of the client, he will often reflect on the past and the dimness of the future. Frustration mounts as he is less able to recover from infections. During this phase the worker must listen and bear witness to the client; offering neither optimistic nor fatalistic scenarios. The client may wish to discuss death and loss, as past relationships are reviewed and he seeks explanations for his fate as part of defence and coping. The client may subtly ask for confirmation of life-decisions made in the past in an attempt to bring meaning to the current situation.

Phase 5. Monitoring and maintaining health status. The client becomes more dependent on the health care system and is helped to accept this.

Phase 6. Supporting close relationships and griefwork. As death becomes imminent, reconnection with significant others, where necessary, becomes vital. The client begins to indicate his awareness of the nearness of death; planning for this may occupy him. The client is supported in these activities.

Phase 7. Caring and advocating for the dying client. Aspects of this are more appropriate to America and it is hoped a worker in this country will not have to negotiate reasonable care with an NHS hospital. The worker may have to support the connection with relatives till the end.

(2) *Those with AIDS Related Complexes (ARC) and Persistent Generalised Lymphadenopathy (PGL)*

These clients will be aware from physical symptoms that they have the virus.

Miller [15] gives a list of the issues in counselling related to seropositivity, which need attention.

(1) Anxiety about having AIDS or the virus.
(2) Depression about the perceived inevitability of infection or developing the full syndrome or both.
(3) Morbid obsession about the disease, ruminations and checking for symptoms.
(4) Guilt about being homosexual and the resurrection of past 'misdemeanours'.
(5) Social, domestic and occupational disruption and stress.

Counselling is necessary to keep anxieties to a minimum and prevent panic attacks. Frankness is necessary, especially in safe sex counselling; if the client does not understand why he should make changes in his sexual behaviour he will not do so, and should understand that these are as much for his own benefit as for potential partners, since any STD will be dangerous. It should be noted that whether ill or recovered, these clients will feel well enough most of the time to conduct a normal life.

A related problem is getting the client to keep in touch with his doctor since such follow-up is unpleasant and can mean hearing at any time that he has AIDS. Acquiring PGL or being told one is seropositive often serves as a catalyst for the ventilation of previously troubling emotional issues within a relationship. The worker must be alert for potentially destructive themes arising in this manner [15].

(3) *Asymptomatic HIV Seropositives*

This is the category of people carrying the virus who have sero-converted and are thus detectable by means of blood tests as having the virus, but show no symptoms and feel quite well. At present not all HIV sero-positives go on to become symptomatics. This group causes some of the greatest problems. As has been said, many arguments have been fought around the test for HIV sero-positivity and this is a group which the medical professions are anxious should be carefully counselled, especially in safe sex practices, since at the moment this group is possibly one of the most dangerous in relation to the spread of the disease. Being told one has a pre-AIDS condition yet show no symptoms whatever must be an extremely anxiety-provoking situation. Anger, and a consequent tendency to react as if nothing was wrong, are possible reactions. There is evidence from some of these men (and from the symptomatic categories as well) that they may go on 'binges' without telling their partners of their condition. The worker who is aware of this may be able to help prevent this, since as well as the danger to the partners there is danger to the client from STDs and from guilt if frank AIDS develops.

(4) *Those Who are Concerned to Reduce Their Risk of Acquiring AIDS. The Worried Well*

Far more common than frank AIDS is the fear of AIDS, from the highly sexually active man who is objectively concerned to reduce his risk of contracting the syndrome, to the man who becomes clinically depressed and anxious about AIDS. The difficulty in distinguishing between early AIDS and anxiety has already been mentioned [18].

Whatever the level of the problem, the first task is to present clear information about the actual degree of risk and the steps that can be taken to reduce it. The chance of contracting AIDS in this country is, at present, small. Miller considers that if the anxiety level is considerable it can lead to significant functional impairment and refers to this as 'pseudo AIDS' [18]. Therefore, the social worker should be alert for psychiatric complications.

(5) *Sufferers of Pre-senile Dementia and Mental Conditions Associated with HTLV III Infection*

One aspect of the virus which appears least known about is the effect on the brain. It is known to lodge there and may cause deterioration of the brain cells leading to a condition of pre-senile dementia. Speaking in Edinburgh in October 1985, Miller [19] suggested that up to 40 per cent of HIV positives may develop neurological deficits, the resulting dementia syndrome involving personality changes, visual difficulties, memory disturbances, poor concentration, ataxia and speech impairments. There are indications that, if the person does not develop frank AIDS, then the dementia will be a long term condition, especially since the sufferers will be young at the onset. There is evidence that those who do not show physical symptoms of HIV infection may eventually succumb to neurological damage.

The implication for social service provision, if these propositions are true, are enormous, since those requiring care for dementia will be young and possibly require many years of care. Many gay men are estranged from their families and will have no system of support on this level and may require long term residential care. For the carers, considerable support will be necessary for those looking after a young loved one who has undergone a personality change. These are the cases which might involve most input from field services, involving considerable resources in the form of home helps, respite care, support-groups, welfare rights, home nursing, etc.

(6) *Intra-venous Drug Users*

This is the most difficult group to help since an IV drug user, on the balance of evidence, when needing to use drugs will risk a dirty needle rather than not use. The most dangerous practice is that of irrigating the syringe by drawing blood into it and flushing it out to wash out all the drug. Specialised counselling from drug rehabilitation agencies is probably the most effective way of dealing with this group.

(7) *Haemophiliacs*

Most of the haemophiliac's attentions are concentrated on his centre which will have social work staff. The field social worker may become involved if the person develops AIDS and will need to take into account the fact that only the usual proportion of these people will be homosexual. Haemophiliacs who are HIV positive will require safe sex counselling and in the case of heterosexual couples this would preclude having children. The Haemophiliac Society is a powerful, well organised pressure group and can be a resource when helping a haemophiliac.

(8) *Pregnant Mothers and Foetae*

The bulk of advice for women who are HIV positive is to avoid pregnancy permanently, especially as there seem to be indications that becoming pregnant can result in the onset of frank AIDS [20]. Further, it is usually suggested that such women who do become pregnant should be counselled on termination; this advice is based on the finding that the virus seems always to be transmitted to the foetus and about 50 per cent of these children will develop frank AIDS within two years of birth.

The question of babies with HIV positivity becomes a social work one especially in the case of IV drug users; these women have always been treated with suspicion when pregnant because of the effects of the virus on the child and the lifestyle which tends to prevent proper ante natal care.

(9) *Heterosexuals as a Group – Additional Comments*

It is usually thought that vaginal sex is safe sex but this is not necessarily the case. A study [20] showed that 36 per cent of heterosexual partners of HIV positives had themselves indications of HIV infection; the rate for homosexuals is 40-50 per cent, thus indicating that the rectum is not much more susceptible than the vagina or cervix to the virus. Recent trends indicate a more rapid increase in infection rates in heterosexual couples.The modes of male/female transmission are now being studied. It is the predominant mode of transmission in Africa and Haiti. The social work intervention is the same as for homosexuals; condoms it would seem work quite well in heterosexual intercourse. A problem for a male heterosexual who has an AIDS condition is that much of the support system is provided for and run by gays. This may prove a considerable strain on his self image and in such groups as Body Positive (support for HIV positives on a self-help basis) he may meet predominantly gays. The social worker may have to provide a great deal of support in this sort of case.

(10) *The Lovers, Families and Friends of Diagnosed AIDS and ARC Clients*

A large number of stable gay couples exist and, when AIDS strikes a partner, the couple has to be looked at together. Miller [15] lists qualitative issues in counselling established lovers of clients with AIDS.

(1) Fear about the possible death of the lover; grief, shock and helplessness.
(2) Fear of becoming infected, leading to anxiety, depression and obsessional worries.
(3) Reduced sexual functioning, especially loss of libido and loss of prospect of future sexual activity.
(4) Guilt about the possibility of having infected the partner and others.
(5) Uncertainty about what to do next; conflict between avoiding infection and love of partner; guilt about this conflict.
(6) Uncertainty about what to do to help the partner.

(7) Clinical anxiety and depression.

The possibility of having been infected is a real worry to the partner. He may be able to nurse his lover, but who will nurse him? The lover will find himself in an unaccustomed role as caretaker and may find himself acting as mediator between his lover, his friends and professionals. The lover may have mixed feelings towards the partner, thus adding a burden of guilt, and the social worker needs to raise this issue with lovers if they do not do it themselves. It is often a great relief for them to know that the feelings are universal and natural. The lover will have to be helped to cope with his grief and anxiety after the death.

Families present a thorny problem as this will possibly be their first realisation of their son's homosexuality. The family may need information on their son's lifestyle to help them understand him. Family therapy may be necessary to improve communication and restore effective links for support.

With friends it is important for the client to maintain as far as possible his friendships. If they are ignorant of the highly specific routes of transmission of the virus, they may avoid the client with consequent damage to his self esteem and social confidence. Gay friends may feel particularly vulnerable and avoid their friend through mixed emotions.

SOCIAL POLICY CONSIDERATIONS

The social worker dealing with people with AIDS will obviously be working closely with the NHS and probably the voluntary sector. The person with AIDS or a related condition will have become medicalised and probably referred by the hospital service for counselling or domiciliary help; the NHS has coped quite well up till now but if there is a significant increase in the number of cases there may be problems in the hospitals. Until now it seems that hospitals have increased the turnover of patients while decreasing the number of beds by reducing the length of stay in hospital, but there is some doubt as to whether some of the conditions related to frank AIDS are susceptible to this technique. Thus if social workers are asked to provide domiciliary services for these people, this may cause problems in certain areas with the reluctance of some workers to go into the homes of people with AIDS [21]. There have been instances of homophobic reactions in the health service together with such reactions as exaggerated precautions against the virus which seems to have more to do with the homosexual label on the patient than the virus. Some dentists are particularly prone to this and are, in some instances, refusing to treat anyone who is gay.

172

The voluntary sector has played a major role in helping people with AIDS, but this did not come from the established conventional voluntary sector but mainly from the networks existing within the gay community and these specialise in the areas of telephone helplines, safe sex advice and support groups. They are often very underfunded and are finding it difficult to get government money but are providing an efficient and fairly comprehensive service throughout the country. There are two main national organisations; the Terrence Higgins Trust based in London and often providing spokespeople in the national media, and the Scottish AIDS Monitor based in Edinburgh. But under these is a network of local organisations, operating telephone helplines and support groups, which the social worker should be aware of in his particular area: the national organisations will advise on these.

CONCLUSION

In conclusion, at present the helper has a fairly difficult task dealing with a stigmatising disease and the fears of those around him as well as his own. Therefore, it is wise to be mindful of the stance of non-judgmentalism in order not to apply these fears to his clients. Notions of guilt or innocence are inappropriate here in relation to the client unless, of course, he brings these feelings to the helper when they must be addressed, such as when he has gone on a sex binge after diagnosis and is now feeling guilt. The emphasis should be on helping the client adjust to the present circumstances and to all categories of client, safe sex advice without moral judgment, not forgetting to practise what he preaches! It should be emphasised that the ordinary skills of a social worker are sufficient to help a person with AIDS and the intent of this paper has been merely a guide to issues which are not immediately obvious.

References

1. Terrence Higgins Trust pamphlet *AIDS and HTLV III Medical Briefing*, October 1985, gives basic information about the virus, disease and safe sex practices.

2. Advice for Social Workers is given in Social Work Services Group Circular No. DSW/1/86 14.1.86 and

3. The best text to date on this subject seems to be: Schoenberg, R., Goldberg, R.S. & Shore, D.A. (Eds.) *With Compassion Towards Some: Homosexuality and Social Work in America.* Harrington Park Press, NY, 1985.

4. De Crescenza, T. & McGill, C. 1978, an unpublished thesis in Decker, B. 'Counselling Gay and Lesbian Couples'. In Schoenberg et al. (3).

5. These figures are based broadly on Kinsey's findings.

6. See, e.g. National Council for Civil Liberties, *Homosexuality and the Social Services*, and Schoenberg et al.(3).

7. Weeks, J. *Sexuality*. Ellis Horwood Tavistock Publications, 1986, particularly chs. 2 and 3.

8. A selection of such literature might include: Freedman, M. *Homosexuality and Psychological Functioning*. Brooks Cole, 1971. Danneker, M. *Theories of Homosexuality*. GMP, London, 1978. Scanzoni, L. & Mollekot, V.R. *Is the Homosexual My Neighbour?* SCM Press, London, 1978.

9. Messing, A.E. et al. 'Confronting Homophobia in the Health Care Setting, Guidelines for Social Work Practice, 1984. In Schoenberg et al.(3).

10. E.g. see *Gay Scotland*. May/June 1985, No.20, p.5. Comment signed by co-ordinators of Scottish AIDS Monitor (SAM).

11. Given at SAM Conference, 'AIDS and its Management', Edinburgh, October, 1985.

12. There have been a number of instances of bad communication here, e.g. *Community Care*. April 17th, 1986, Terry Cotton, Fulhams Health Coordinator describes such instances.

13. Terrence Higgins Trust and SAM provide a range of leaflets on safe sex.

14. Green, J. 'Counselling HTLV III Sero-positives'. In Miller, D., Weber, J. & Green, J. *The Management of AIDS Patients*. Macmillan, London, 1986, ch. 8.

15. Miller, D. & Green, J. 'Psychological Support and Counselling for Patients with AIDS' *Genitourinary Medicine*. 61, 1985, 273-278.

16. Kubler-Ross, E. *On Death and Dying*. Macmillan, London, 1969.

17. Lopez, D.J. & Getzel, G.S. 'Helping Gay Aids Patients in Crisis' *Social Casework*. Sept. 1984, 387-394.

18. Miller, D. et al. 'A "Pseudo AIDS" Syndrome Following from Fear of AIDS' *British Journal of Psychiatry*. 146, 1985, 550-551.

19. Given at SAM Conference, 'AIDS and its Management'. Edinburgh, October 1985.

20. AIDS & ARC, Social Work Resource Centre, School of Social Work, University of Cardiff, 1986.